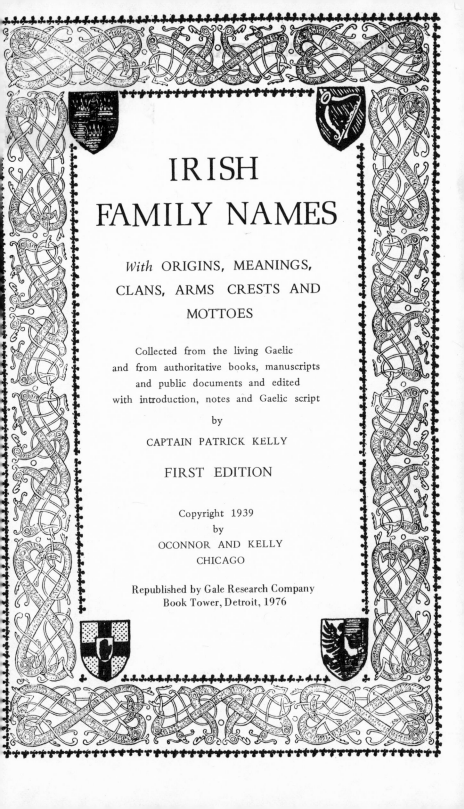

IRISH
FAMILY NAMES

With ORIGINS, MEANINGS, CLANS, ARMS CRESTS AND MOTTOES

Collected from the living Gaelic
and from authoritative books, manuscripts
and public documents and edited
with introduction, notes and Gaelic script

by

CAPTAIN PATRICK KELLY

FIRST EDITION

Copyright 1939
by
OCONNOR AND KELLY
CHICAGO

Republished by Gale Research Company
Book Tower, Detroit, 1976

**Library of Congress
Cataloging in Publication Data**

Kelly, Patrick, 1893-
　　Irish family names.

　　Reprint of the ed. published by O'Connor and Kelly,
Chicago.
　　Bibliography: p.
　　Includes index.
　　1. Names, Personal--Irish.　2. Heraldry--Ireland.
I. Title.
CS2415.K4　　1976　　929.4'09415　　75-23446
ISBN 0-8103-4146-8

Contents

INTRODUCTION

CLANS

The clan system of Ireland was well established in pre-Christian times and the evolution of the clan structure fostered the early use of permanent Irish family names. Some of these surnames are recorded as being in existence before the 7th century and most of them were well established before the end of the 12th century.

Because clan affiliations are historically important in relation to the surnames recorded in this book a brief discussion of the clan will be of value to the reader. The clan was a natural growth from or around an outstanding individual or family. Consequently the clan name was usually formed by the addition of a prefix or suffix to the foundation name. Thus, the prefixes, Cineal, Clann, Corca, Muintear, Siol, Slioght, Tallach, Ui, Dal, and the suffixes *-acht, -na, -ne, -raighe*, are all synonymous with the English words *race, progeny, family, descendants, etc.* Exceptional prefixes are *Tuath, Aos, Pobul,* (people) and *Feara,* (men). Examples: *Cineal Aodha,* (race of Aodh), *Clann Colmain,* (race of Colman), *Corca Seachlann,* (race of Seachlann), *Muintear Eoluis,* (family of Eolus), *Siol Anmchadha,* (seed of Anmchadha), *Ui Maine* (descendants of Maine), *Cianaght* (race of Cian), *Feara Bile* (men of Bile).

In effect the clan was a distinct political entity with a large measure of political freedom, self reliance and self sufficiency. It had its own territory, its own judges, priests and historians. Subject to the limitations of the national code it had its own laws. Its leadership was sometimes hereditary, sometimes elective within a ruling family. Property essential to life was held in common but personal ownership of things personally created or inherited was recognized. Allegiance and service to the national government under the Ard-Ri were loosely implemented thru chieftains, princes and provincial kings. The religion of this state was a polytheistic paganism supported by and supporting the druids and promising immortality in Tir-na-h-oige (land of Youth), a heaven world on the order of the Norse Valhalla. The fifth century Gallo-Roman missionary Patrick and his assistants effected a gentle transition from this paganism to Christianity without greatly changing the existing social and political structure of the nation. So the clan system survived under Christianity, withstood the shock of the Norse invasions and lingered on thru several centuries of the Irish struggle against England until the wholesale seizure of clan lands and execution or banishment of leaders after the Jacobite-Orange war. Even then, in Gaelic speaking western Ireland vestiges of the clans survived and continue in existence today. The best that can be said for the clan system is that it fostered family loyalty, romance and some of the spiritual values. The worst that can be said against it is that inherently it militated against national solidarity.

FAMILY NAMES

At the outset when the clans were not numerous or large the clan name also served the purpose of a surname and, with the personal name, was sufficient for personal identification within and outside the clan. As the clans grew in size and subclans and septs were established these too took name from the personal names of their founders. Gradually some of these sept names became more or less permanent family names and, in line with this custom, permanent surnames began to appear in Ireland as early as the 8th century, became increasingly prevalent in succeeding years and were widely established before the end of the 13th century. As previously mentioned, surnames were not generally adopted in other European countries until much later. Some authorities state that most Irish surnames became fixed by royal ordinance in the reign of King Brian Boru, 1002-1014. While it is admitted that the custom spread rapidly during Brian's reign there is no documentary or inferential evidence in support of this statement. On the contrary, Brian's own family had no permanent surname. The appelation *Boru* (of the tribute of cattle) was in association with his exploitation of certain features of the Seancas Mor (national law, erroneously named the Brehon code). The surname O'Brien was established by his grandchildren.

The first Irish surnames were formed by prefixing the word Ua, (O), *descended from,* to the genitive form of the personal name of a paternal ancestor, generally the grandfather. Thus: *O Flainn,* descended from Flann (the red), anglicized O Flynn.

Later Irish surnames and most Scottish surnames were formed by prefixing Mac (son) to the genitive of the personal name of the father; thus: MacMahon, MacDomnaill. The surnames of women have the prefix *Ni* (abbreviation of *ingean* daughter). Thus: *Sadv Ni Flainn,* Sabina Flynn. With Mrs. and Miss the regular name prefix is used; thus: Ban O Ceallaigh, Mrs. (wife of) Kelly, Ingean Mac Cartha, Miss (daughter of) McCarthy. There were of course some exceptions, notably in connection with some of the Norman-Irish families which became established after the first Anglo-Norman invasion. The prefix *Fitz* (from Norman-French *fils,* son) is essentially of Norman origin, altho it has sometimes been borrowed for anglicization of some purely Gaelic names.

Since most of our surnames come from the personal name of some ancestor a discussion of the nature and meaning of such personal names is pertinent. These were sometimes descriptive of some mental or physical attribute or qualification, as *Flann* (ruddy), *Tadg* (philosopher). Sometimes they were from the names of animals having characteristics of strength, endurance or devotion admired by the old warriors and hunters, such as *Mahon* (the bear), *Felan* (little wolf). Some were occupational. Not a few were from the gods of the Celtic pantheon, as Arth, Aodh and Aongus. After the fifth century some of the names of Christian saints began to appear but these were comparatively rare and always in combination with a Gaelic prefix such as Giolla Padraig (servant or guide of St. Patrick), Maol Iosa (devoted to Jesus).

In general the foregoing were the types of personal names from which purely Gaelic surnames were derived. In addition there were some Norse personal names such as Olaf and a good many Norman-French names such as de Burgo contributed by Danish and early Anglo-Norman invaders whose descendants were absorbed into native population. Since the family names derived from these were first founded in Ireland they are rightfully classed with the Irish surnames in these pages. It is worthy of mention here that all those who arrived in Ireland prior to the time of Henry VIII became part of the Irish nation. English invaders coming thereafter were not assimilated.

For the convenience of the reader each surname is grouped with its coat of arms in the following order:
1. Surname is Gaelic type.
2. Surname is Gaelic script.
3. The various anglicized forms which have evolved from the Gaelic name together with such translated forms as have been attempted.
4. Origin, clan affiliation, meaning and history.
5. Motto.
6. Footnote showing translation of the Gaelic root word.

Some well-known Irish names will not be found herein, not because they are not truly Gaelic in origin but rather because no coat or arms pertaining to them seems to be recorded. Yet other names may not be found spelled in their present form but a search will reveal their origin.

COATS OF ARMS

For hundreds of years before Christianity the leaders of the Celtic clans assembled at Teacmor Tabartha (Tara Hall) when it became necessary to elect rulers or to discuss the law. Before these assemblies proceeded to their order of business it was necessary that the Tract of the Law (Seancas Mor) be read and before such reading could take place the shield of each attending clan was placed over the seat of the clan leader. On these shields were symbols of the achievements of the clans and from them evolved the clan and family coats of arms. In later centuries many of the Gaelic mottoes were translated into Latin and yet later others were translated into Norman-French in line with the heraldic practices of those years. But many of the original symbols and mottoes persist. The Red Hand of Ulster is one of these. It is symbolic of an occurrence incidental to the first landing of the Celtic race on Irish soil. Another is the lion which symbolizes an actual or legendary exploit of a Celtic leader antedating the Celtic invasion of Ireland. Yet another is the oft depicted serpent, a symbol of eternity in pagan Celtic mythology. Other symbols have to do with the deeds or fortunes of clans or individuals in later years. In fact some of the bearings depicted on the shields shown here mark the achievements or adventures on foreign soil of clan leaders expatriated during the long sustained struggle for Irish independence. The Coats of Arms shown herein are those which Heraldry generally associates with the surnames found grouped with them. The most reliable of accepted authorities have been studied in this connection. Where two or more escutcheons appear as pertaining to one surname the one associated with the most important clan or house is shown.

REFERENCES:

Irish State Papers, Henry VIII, Edward VI, Mary, Elizabeth and James I; Irish Patent Rolls of James I; Annals of Ireland by the Four Masters, Owen Connellan; Transactions of the Ossory Archaelogical Society; Cambrensis Eversus, M. Kelly; The O Connors of Connaught, C. O. O Connor; History of Ireland, Geoffrey Keating; History of Sligo, T. O Rourke; Clan O Toole and Leinster Septs, P. L. O Toole; The Cromwellian Settlement of Ireland, J. P. Prendergast; Memoirs of Armagh City, James Stuart; Ireland's Ancient Schools and Scholars, J. Healy; Celtic Ireland by E. MacNeill; Proceedings of the Royal Irish Academy; Manx Names, A. W. Moore; Tain Bo Cuailne, Joseph Dunn; A Chronicle of Irish Affairs, Hennessy; Irish Names and Places, P. W. Joyce; The Martyrology of Tallaght, M. Kelly; Genealogical Manuscripts and Annals of Ireland, Dubhallrach M. Firbisigh (edited by O Donovan); Annals of Clonmacnoise; Manuscript Materials of Ancient Irish History, Eugene O Curry; O Kelly's Country, Customs of Ui Maine, John O Donovan; Genealogies, and Customs of Ui Fiachrach, John O Donovan; Sloinnte Gael is Gall, P. Woulfe; Genealogical Tracts, Thorlough O Rafferty; Leabhar na gCeart; Annals of the Kingdom of Ireland; Miscellany of the Irish Archaeological Society; The Book of Lecan; The Book of Ui Maine; Grammar of the Irish Language, John O Donovan; Leabhar na Laoihea, J. J. O Kelly; History of Clare, James Frost; History of Galway, James Hardiman; Municipal Documents of Ireland (1172-1320), John T. Gilbert; The Black Book of Limerick, J. MacCaffrey; Pacata Hibernia, S. O. Grady; Publications of the Irish Texts Society; Fiorsgeal na h-Eireann; O Hart's Irish Pedigrees; Burke's Peerage; The Oireachtas Lists of the Gaelic League; Statutes of the 1367 Parliament of Kilkenny, translated by James Hardiman from manuscript in the British Museum; Book of Ballymote; Publications and Manuscripts of the Royal Irish Academy.

ó eꞇꞇıᵹeꞇꞇꞇꞇ, ó eꞇꞇıᵹeıꞇꞇ, ó eıcꞇꞇıᵹeıꞇꞇ

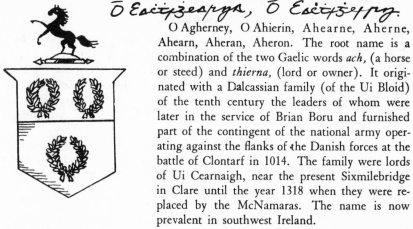

O Agherney, O Ahierin, Ahearne, Aherne, Ahearn, Aheran, Aheron. The root name is a combination of the two Gaelic words *ach,* (a horse or steed) and *thierna,* (lord or owner). It originated with a Dalcassian family (of the Ui Bloid) of the tenth century the leaders of whom were later in the service of Brian Boru and furnished part of the contingent of the national army operating against the flanks of the Danish forces at the battle of Clontarf in 1014. The family were lords of Ui Cearnaigh, near the present Sixmilebridge in Clare until the year 1318 when they were replaced by the McNamaras. The name is now prevalent in southwest Ireland.

> Ꞇıᵹeꞇꞇꞇꞇ, *g. id. (smt.* -n), *pl.* -í, *m.,* a lord, a master, a proprietor
>
> eꞇċ, *g.* eıċ, *pl. id.,* eꞇcꞇ *coll.), m.,* a horse, a steed

O Ꞙꞇıꞁíꞇ

O Hallyn, Hallin, Hallion, Allin and Allen. The original name is the diminutive form of the Gaelic word *aill* (a rock, cliff or granite mass). The origin is unknown but ancient and came from a personal name. It is now found chiefly in Offaly and Ormond.

> ꞇıꞁꞁ, -e, *pl. id.,* ꞇꞁꞁꞇꞇꞇ and ꞇıꞁꞇꞇeꞇċꞇ a cliff, a rock

FORTIS ET FIDELIS

mꞇc ꞇoꞇᵹuıs, mꞇc ꞇoꞇᵹusꞇ

McEnnesse, McHinchey, McNisse, MacEnnis, MacInnes, MacInch, MacKinch, MacHinch, MacNeese, MacNiece, MacNish, Mannice, Minnish, Ennis, Innes and Hinchey. The root name is composed of the two Gaelic words *aon* (one) and *guish* (choice). Being of ancient Gaelic origin it is also prevalent in Scotland, particularly in Argyleshire. In Scotland it is generally anglicized Angus and McAngus.

> ꞇoꞇᵹuꞇ, -ꞇ, -uıꞇ, *m.,* Aonghus, the Irish god of love; *al.* ꞇ. ꞇꞇ �9ꞇoᵹꞇ, ꞇ. mꞇc ꞇꞇ Ꞇꞇᵹóꞇ.

Ó bearsa

Ó beapẓa.

O Barrie, O Barry, Barrie, Barry, O Barr, Barr. The original name is from the Gaelic word *bearr-gacht,* (diligence). The family furnished chiefs to a clan in Iveross in the barony of Kenry, County Limerick. Formerly a branch of this family was seated in Tirawley, County Mayo. According to O'Donovan this branch is now extinct. There is no reason to confuse this name or family with the Norman-Irish family of *de Barry.* The motto is old French and means "Drink first."

beaṗẓaċt, -a, *f.,* diligence

barún

bapúṇ.

Baroun, Baron, Barron. This name was transplanted to Ireland soon after the original Anglo-Norman invasion. The transplanted family were merchants of standing in Dublin as early as the year 1200. A branch of the Fitzgeralds of Kilkenny assumed the family name of Barron and thence it became prevalent in Kilkenny, Waterford and Tipperary. The coat of arms pertains to this last named family. Its Latin motto means "Fortune favors the brave."

Ó beardín

Ó beapáṇ

O Barrane, O Barran, Barrane, Barron, (Barnes, Barrington). The root name is from the old Gaelic word *barrawnai* (fomenter of strife) and not, as some authorities hold, from the Gaelic word meaning a spear. The name is that of two old families, one of Thomond and one of Tirconnell. The French motto freely translated means "I am the same during my life."

beaṗṗánaiḋe, *g. id., pl.* -óċe, a fomentor of strife

Ó beiġ   Ó beaġáin

Ó beiġ, Ó beaġáiny.

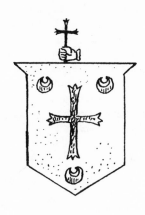

O Begg, Begg, Beggs, Biggs, O Beggin, Beggan, Biggin, Biggins, Biggy, O Beggahan, Begaddon, Begane, O Begane, Biganne, and sometimes translated Little and Littleton. The root name and its three variants come from the Gaelic word *begg* (small). The name has existed in various clans since the thirteenth century and is widely scattered but is most prevalent in Limerick and Clare.

beaġ, *gsf.* biġe, *comp.* luġa, *u.,* little, small, tiny, few ; minor, in place

mac ḟeóRaiṡ, mac ḟeóRuiṡ

mac ḟeópaiṡ, mac ḟeópuiṡ.

McOrish McHorish, McKeorish, McCorish, McKeoris, Korish, Corish, Birmingham, Bermingham. Irish and English variants of the original name MacFeorish which was assumed by the Norman Irish family founded by the Norman, Pierce or Peter de Birmingham.

Ó bláṫṁaic

Ó bláṫṁaṡc.

Blawick, Blowick, Blouk, and (incorrectly) Blake. The root name is formed from the two Gaelic words *blah* (blossom) and *mac* (son). It was common in Mayo in the 15th century but later was gradually merged into Blake. The Blakes were high sheriffs of Connaught in the early part of the 14th century.

bláṫ, *g.* bláiṫ, *pl.* bláṫa, bláṫanna and bláiṫe, *m.,* a bloom, blossom, flowerbud, flower

4

Ó beolláin, Ó beollárg.

O Beollaine, O'Beolane, O Bowlane, O Bolan, Bolan, Boland, Bowland. Descended from *Bjolan*, an old Norse name. This family is of Viking origin. Its fusions created many important houses in Ireland such as: (1) A Sligo family, the heads of which were erenaghs or traditional stewards of the Columban church lands of Drumcliffe. (2) A Delcassian family in Clare and south Thomond which was affiliated with the MacMahons, descendants of Mahon of the race of Brian Boru.

Ó baoigeallain, Ó baoigeallárg.

O Boylane, O Boylan, Boylan, a diminutive form of the next name below and thus meaning *descendant of the little apprehensive one*. This was the name of an Ulster family who were chiefs of all Oriel in early Christian Ireland and later of Dartraighe, the present barony of Dartry in County Monaghan. Ó baoigill, Ó baoigill

O Boyle and Boyle. The root name is from the Gaelic word *bweel*, (peril or apprehension). The O Boyles were early chiefs of the Three Tuaths in Donegal, being among the leaders of Cinel Connaille and of the same clan as the O Donnells and O Doughertys. They were later supplanted in their territory by the MacSweeneys and then became chiefs of Tir-Ainmhireach in western Donegal, now known as the barony of Boylagh. They are mentioned in The Annals of the Four Masters and The Fiants of Elizabeth as·being actively engaged in the defensive warfare of the Irish against the forces òf Elizabeth. In those years the fortunes of war dispersed them thruout the island. Their Latin motto means "The Lord will provide."

baoġal, -ail, *pl. id.* and -lta, *m.*, danger ;
a point open to attack ; apprehension .

Ó buaḋacáin, Ó buaḋacárg.

O Boughane, O Boughan, O Boghan, Boughan, Bougan, Boohan, Bowen and Bohanan. The root name is from the diminutive form of the Gaelic word *booach* (victorious). The name originated amongst the clans of Thomond in the 13th century and later became prevalent in Kerry, Tipperary, Offaly and Kilkenny. The translation of the Latin motto is "Strong in faith and war."

buaḋaċ, -aiġe, *a.*, victorious ; valuable.

Ó bReacáin, Ó bpeacóʑʑ.

O Breckan, O Brackan and Brackan, from the Gaelic word *brack* (piebald). This is an old family of Offaly not widely prevalent or numerous.

bʀeac, *gsf.* bʀice, *a.*, speckled, spotted

Ó bROLCáin   Ó bROILeacáin
Ó bpolćóʑʑ,   Ó bpoʑleacóʑʑ.

O Brallaghan, O Brollaghan, Brollaghan and Bradley. The basic name is from the Gaelic *brollac,* a breast, chest or breastwork and (by inference) means *one who constitutes himself a breastwork or defender.* The original family was located in Ulster and was descended from Suibhne Meann, a 7th century King of Ireland. Their location was in Clogher, County Tyrone, whence they later moved to the vicinity of Derry. O Healy's "Ancient Schools and Scholars" makes frequent mention of numerous illustrious bearers of this name. O Brelligan, O Brilleghane, O Brilehan are also common variants of this name.

bʀollać, -aiʒ, *pl. id.* and -aiʒe, *m.*, the breast, the bosom; a breast-work.

Ó bRaDacáin, Ó bpaDacóʑʑ.

O Bradaghan, Bradekin, Bradican, Bradagan, Braddigan, Brodigan, from the diminutive form of the Gaelic word *bradhac,* (spirited). In the 14th century the name and its root names below numbered powerful families in Mayo and Roscommon.

Ó bRáDaiʒ Ó bpaDaiʒ.

O Brady, Brady, "descendant of the spirited fellow." (See last previous name.) The Latin motto means "Virtue conquers dangers."

Ó bRaDáin Ó bpaDáʑʑ.

O Bradane, O Bradan, O Bradden, Bradan, Bradden and sometimes translated Salmon from the Gaelic word *bradawn* (a spirited fish, a salmon). Leaders of a Roscommon sept contemporary with the Bradys and Braddigans, which see above.

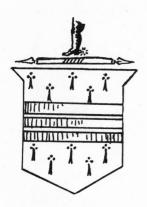

Ó bRαnαζάin

Ó bpαγαζαρρ.

O Branagan, O Branigan, O Brengan, Branagan, Branigan, Brannigan, Brennigan, Brangan, Brankin. The root name is the diminutive form of the Gaelic word *bran* (a raven). The family formed part of the Cinel Eoghain in Derry.

bṗαn, -αin, *pl. id., m.,* a raven.

Ó bReαsαil

Ó bpeαραρl.

O Breassell, O Brazil, Brassill, Brazil, Brazel, from the northern Celtic *breasalach* (truculence). This is a very old and a very scattered Irish name. See Breslin.

bṗéαṗlαċ, raving ; foaming

Ó bReisleáin, Ó bReislein

Ó bpeρρleάṗy, Ó bpeρρleṗy

O Breslane, Breslane, Breslaun, Breslin. A diminutive form of *breasal* (see above) and with the same general meaning. This family was part of Cinel Enda and its heads were chiefs of Fanad in Donegal from the 10th to the 13th century when they migrated to Fermanagh and became brehons to the Maguires. One of their branches succeeded the O Brennan as erenaghs of the church lands of Derryvullen. Another branch furnished chiefs of Kinanley and yet another belonged to the Ui Fiachrach.

Ó bRaoın, Ó bpaofy.

O Braoin, O Brean, O Breen, O Bruen, Breen, Bruen. From the Gaelic *braon* (sorrow or wretchedness). The name originated with the family of Maine, son of King Niall of the Nine Hostages. It numbered many important groups as early as the 10th century. The following are the most known. (a) O Breen of Westmeath, lords of Brawney where the name is still prevalent. (b) O Breen of Meath where, according to The Annals of the Four Masters, they were chiefs of Luighne down to the year 1201. (c) O Breen of Roscommon who were erenaghs of the church of St. Coman, and of whom was Tigearnach O Braoin, the annalist.

bpóın, *g.* bpóın, *pl.* bpóntƆ, *m.,* grief, sorrow

Ó bRaonáın, Ó bpaogáfy.

O Brenane, O Brennan, O Brinane, Brennan, Brinane, Brinan. A diminutive form of the Gaelic *braon* and therefore the translation is "descended from the little sorrowful one." There were several distinct families of this name. O Brennan of Ossory who were chiefs of Ui Duach in northern Kilkenny. O Brennan of Westmeath, chiefs of Clan Crevagh. O Brennan of Kerry, chiefs of Dunkerron and followers of O Sullivan Mor. O Brennan of Galway, affiliated with the O Madden. The motto is "In this sign conquer."

mac an bReıteaman.

mac an bpeıteanfay

McAbreham, McEbrehowne, McEvrehune, McEvrehoona, McEvrehon, McBrehuna, McBrehon, McVrehoune, Brehony, Breheny, Brohoon and sometimes translated "Judge." From the Gaelic *breihiv* (judge or lawgiver). The various groups of this name are descended from the great brehon families or hereditary judges of the ancient political structure of Eire. The name is now generally prevalent, especially in Connaught and west Ulster.

bpeıteamóƆ, *indec. a.,* juƆıcıal,

Ó bRıc, Ó bpıc.
Ó bRuıc Ó bpuıc.

O Brick, Brick, O Bruck from the genitive form of the Gaelic word *brock* (a badger). The family originated in the Clan Dalcass, in Clare in the 11th century and established itself in Kerry and in Waterford where its leaders where rulers of the southern Decies. bpoc, *g.* bpuıc, a badger

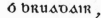

Ó bRUAÓAIR,

Ó bṗuaṫaiṗ.

O Bruadar, O Brouder, O Broder, O Brother, Brouder, Broder, Brooder, Bruder, Brother, Brauders, Brodders, Broderick. From the old Gaelic word *bruador* (a dream or reverie), possibly this word came into the Gaelic with an early Norse invasion. There were four distinct families of this name. O Bruadar of Galway, followers of the O Kelly up to the 16th century and still numerous there. O Bruadar of Ossory who were chiefs of Iverk. O Bruadar of Innishowen in Donegal. O Bruadar of Cork to which belonged the O Bruadars of Limerick. For further information on these families see McLean's introduction to the Poems of David O Bruadair, published by the Irish Texts Society. The Latin motto is: "From the spear a crown."

bṗuaṫaṗ, -aiṗ, *pl. id., m.,* a dream, a reverie; bṗuaṫaiṗ, *f.*

mac bRUAIÓeAÓA,

mac bṗuaiṫeaṫa.

McBrouddie, McBroudy, McBrodie, MacBrody, Brody and Brodie. The root name is a form of the Gaelic word *bruaid* (a fragment or morsel), hence, a little fellow. The MacBrodys were hereditary bards and historians to the O Briens of Thomond, from whom they held the properties of Ballybrody, Kilkeedy and Lettermoylan in Clare. They figured importantly in early Irish literature. Conor MacBrody was one of those who approved The Annals of the Four Masters. Their estates were confiscated by Cromwell in 1642. The motto is "United."

bṗuaiṫ, -e, *f.,* a fragment; a morsel.

Ó bROŠÁIn-, *Ó bṗóǵaiṗ.*

O Brogane, O Brogan, Brogan. The root word is the diminutive form of the Gaelic word *broa,* (sorrowful). The name originated in Donegal in the 11th century. Its heads were in possession of most of the barony of Carra in Mayo.

bṗónaiǵe, *g. id., f.,* sadness

ᴅᴇ ᴅúʀᴄ, ᴅᴇ ᴅúʀᴄᴀ, *ᴅᴇ bú*ʀᴄ, *ᴅᴇ búʀᴄᴀ*

de Burgo, De Burgh, Bourke, Burke. Descended from William Fitz Adelm de Burgo who came to Eire with the Norman English invasion in 1171 and succeeded Strongbow as governor of that part of Ireland then conquered by the invaders. By a series of marriage alliances with Irish and Norman-Irish families in the succeeding years the Burkes became one of the most powerful Norman-Irish families. When they attained to the lordship of Connaught they adopted the brehon code and proclaimed themselves chieftains under the names MacWilliam Iochtar and MacWilliam Uachtar, i. e., lower and upper MacWilliam. Other and minor branches of the family assumed names from their immediate forebears, such as MacSeonin, MacGibbon and MacRedmond. The motto is "One faith, one king, one law."

ᴏ ᴅᴜᴀᴄᴀʟʟᴀ, *ó ᴅᴜᴀᴄᴀʟʟᴀ.*

O Boughelly, O Bowhilly, O Bohelly, Boughla, Buhilly, Buckley, from the Gaelic *buachill* (a boy or youth). A sixteenth century surname in Cork and Tipperary. The motto is "Neither rashly nor timidly."

> ᴅᴜᴀᴄᴀɪʟʟ, -ᴀʟʟᴀ, -í, *m.*, a boy, a servant-boy, a lad; a servant; a cow-boy, a herd-boy; an unmarried young man

ó ᴅʀᴏɪɴ, *ó ᴅʀᴏᴊᴊ.*

O Birne, O Byrne, Byrne, Byrnes, Byron, Burns. The root name being a form of the Gaelic word *bran* (a raven). The family originated with Bran, son of Maolmorra, King of Leinster who, according to The Annals of the Four Masters, died at Cologne in 1052. Their territory was that of Ui Faolain in northern Kildare whence they were driven by the Anglo-Normans after which they went into the Wicklow mountains where they led the Wicklow clans in warfare against England for four hundred years. Their lands were called Crioch Branach or "Burns' End" and comprised the Barony of Newcastle and part of Arklow and Ballinacor. From the Ranalagh branch of the family came Fiach Mac Hugh O Byrne who so vehemently opposed Elizabeth. The motto of the family is "I have fought and conquered."

ᴅʀᴀɴ raven

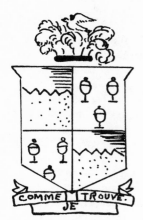

ⱱe ⱱuıⱦıléıⱤ, ⱱe ⱱuıⱦléıⱤ,

ɑe ⱱuıⱦꝉéꝼꝼ, ⱱe ⱱuıⱦꝉéꝼꝼ.

Butler. From the Norman-French *le Buitilier*. The name originated with Theobald Walter who was appointed chief Butler, (minister of economy?) of conquered territory in Ireland by Henry II. He also ruled over the territories of upper and lower Ormond. His family became one of the most important of the Anglo-Norman groups in Ireland. Their French motto may be fully translated "I take things as I find them."

Ó caⱦáın, *Ō Caⱦaꝼꝼ.*

Ó Caghane, Ó Cahaine, Ó Cahane, Ó Kahane, Ó Kaane, Ó Cahan, Ó Caughan, Ó Kane, Ó Keane, Cahane, Cahan, Cane, Cain, Kane, Keane. The root name is from the plural form of the Gaelic *cath,* (battle). The family was a branch of Cinel Eoghan, lords of Keenaght and owners of part of Derry. Their estates were confiscated in the English plantation of Ulster. A branch of the family became assimilated with the Ui Fiachrach in Galway and another branch rose to power in Thomond thru affiliation with the Dalcassians. Available records indicate that the surname was well established in the 11th century.

Caⱦ, -ᴀ, *pl. id.,* -ᴀí and -ᴀnnᴀ, *m.,* a battle, a war; a temptation; strife.

Ó caⱦaıꝉ

Ō Caⱦaꝼꝛ.

Ó Cahill, Cahill, from the Gaelic *cahall,* (valorous or powerful in battle). The name originated in the 8th century from a popular personal name. The more important families of this name were: Ó Cahill of west Galway who were of the race of Ó Shaughnessy; Ó Cahill of east Galway; Ó Cahill of Tipperary, who gave its name to Ballycahill; Ó Cahill of Loch Lein and Ó Cahill of Corofin (Clare), who were of the sept Ui Flaithri.

Caⱦᴀ, *a., gs.* of Caⱦ, battlɩᴇ. warlike.

O Cíaráin, Ó Cjapáfy.

O Kearane, O Kerrane, O Kieran, Kearon, Kearn, Keern, Kierans, Kearons, Kerans, Kerons, Kearns, Kerns, Cairns. The original name is from the Gaelic *keer* or *ciar*, (dark brown or dark colored, swarthy, etc.). Originating with a Tirconnell family in Donegal in the 11th century, branches of which became leaders of septs in Donegal, it spread into Mayo where it was of importance in the 16th century. Later it became widely prevalent. The motto is "Faithful and constant."

Cíap-óubán, -áin, *pl. id., m.,* a person of dark features.

Ó catasaíз, Ó Caíapáíз.

O Cahessy, O Casey, Casey. From the Gaelic word *cahasach* meaning watchful. Therefore it may be translated *descendant of the vigilante or sentinel.* The name had its origin in ancient Meath where the O Caseys were rulers of Saithne (part of present County of Dublin) until defeated by Sir Hugh de Lacy after the Anglo-Norman invasion. Branches of the family became seated in other parts of ancient Ireland, such as: (1) O Casey of Fermanagh, erenaghs of Devinish; (2) O Casey of Mayo, erenaghs of Dunfeeny; (3) O Casey of Roscommon, erenaghs of Cloondara; (4) O Casey of Cork; (5) O Casey of Limerick, coarbs of Coshlea. The motto is "Thru many difficulties."

Caíċípeaċ, -ríѕe, *a.,* wakeful.

Ó ceallacáín, Ó Ceallacáfy.

O Callaghan, O Callahan, Callaghan, Callahan, Calligan. The name is a diminutive of the old Celtic word *ceallach,* meaning contention (not to be confused with a somewhat similar word in middle Gaelic which means "of the church"). It originated with Ceallahain, son of Cashel, king of Munster in the 10th century. The O Callahans were originally chiefs of Cinel Aodha, now Kinalea, in southern Cork. They were overcome in the Anglo-Norman invasion and were driven to the banks of the Blackwater where they established a territory known as Pobul Ui Cheallachain. After the Cromwellian war the head of the family was transferred to Clare. Their motto is "Faithful and bold."

Ceallaċ war, contention

Ó huaruisce, Ófllapufrce.

O Horiske, Hourisky, Horisky, Watters, Waters, Coldwell, Caldwell. The root name is comprised of the two Gaelic words *fuar* (cold) and *uishke,* (water). The name was once common in Ireland.

fuar, -aire, *a.,* cold, chilly

uirce, *g. id., pl.* -cí and -cróeacá, *m.,* water, a water or river

Ó catláin, Ó Catláfy.

O Callaine, O Collhane, O Callan, Culhane, Callan, Callen, Callin, Cawlin, Clahane, Culhane, Clehane. The name consists of the two Gaelic words *cath,* (battle) and *lonn,* (fierce or brave). Therefore the translation is *descendant of the fierce in war.* The name is common in most of Eire. cataíbe, *g. id., pl.* -óte, *m.,* a warrior

lonn, *gsf.* loinne, luinne, *a.,* strong, impetuous, ardent, rapturous, brave, fierce, severe

Ó ceannoubáin, Ó Ceayyoubáfy.

O Cannovane, O Canavan, O Kennavain, Cannavan, Canavan, Kinavan. It is made up of the two Gaelic words *ceann,* (head or top) and *dhuv,* (black), the diminutive suffix *ain* being added. The name originated in Connaught in the 10th century. The family were hereditary physicians to the clans of which the O Flahertys were chiefs. The termination is sometimes mistaken for *bawn,* (white). This accounts for the erroneous translation to Whitehead.

ceann, head. oub, black

Ó canannáin, Ó Cayanyáfy,
Ó canann, Ó Cayayy.

O Cananan, O Conanan, O Cannan, O Cannon, Cannon, Cannan, Canning. The root name is from the Gaelic *cana,* (wolf cub). The family were rulers of Tirconnell from the 9th to the 13th century when they were superseded by the O Donnells.

cana, -ann, *f.,* a wolf cub, a whelp

O CAIRDRE,

Ó Coippbpe.

O Carbery, O Carbry, Carbery, Carbry, Garberry
From the Gaelic word for charioteer. The name
originated in Westmeath in the 11th century
where its founders were chiefs of the territory
coterminous with the present barony of Clon-
lonan.

> Caippbpe, g. id., m., a personal name
> signifying charioteer

O CIARDA, Ó Cpapóa.

O Kerry, O Kirry, Keery, Keary, Karey, Carey.
From the Gaelic keer or ciar, (black). See Kearns.
The name originated with a family of the southern
Ui Neill who ruled Cairbre in Kildare before the
Anglo-Norman invasion. It is common in Meath,
Westmeath, Kildare and thruout Munster. The
motto is "Without stain."

> Cíoṗ, m., jet ; orig. cíoṗ, g. ceáṗa ; obs.
> except in compds., e.g., cíoṗ-óuḃ, jet
> black

O CEARMADA, Ó Ceaṗṁaóa.

O Carmody, O Kermody, Carmody, Kermody.
The name is a combination of the two Gaelic
words ciar, (black) and madha an older form of
the word "madhra" meaning hunting dog or re-
triever. The name has been in existence since the
9th century. It is common today in Clare and
Limerick.

> maóṗaó, g. -aió, pl. -aióe and -aí, m.,
> a dog, a mastiff ; m. piaóaíg, a beagle ;

O CEARNAIŠ, Ó Ceaṗṗaíṡ

O Carney, O Kearney, Carney, Kearney. From
the Gaelic word meaning victorious in battle. The
name first came into existence as a family name
in the early part of the 12th century. There were
several families, principal of which were: (a)
O Kearney of Cashel, members of the Dal Cas;
(b) O Kearney of Mayo, members of the Ui
Fiachrach; (c) O Kearney of Derry, erenaghs of
church lands in that territory.

> Ceáṗnaó, m., act of conquering, con-
> suming.

Ó CARRA, *Ō Cappa.*

O Carra, O Carr, O Karr, Carr, Karr, Kerr. The original name is from the Gaelic word which anciently meant a *spear* or *pointed object* but in modern Gaelic admits of much wider interpretation. The Annals of Ulster and those of The Four Masters show the form "O Cairre." There were many leaders of the name in Galway in the 14th century. The French motto may be freely translated: "All for the right."

> Capp (cappa, cápp), g. caippe, d. caipp spear, a lance, *al.* a pike staff, a shaft.

Ó cearḃaill, *Ō Cearḃaṫll.*

O Carrowill, O Carwell, O Carvill, O Carroll, Carroll, Carvill. The root of the name is in the Gaelic word *cearvh,* meaning a hart or stag. (Latin Cervus) This was a very common ancient Celtic personal name. There are several distinct families of which the following are the most important: O Carroll of Ely, from Cearbaill of Eile who fought at Clontarf. The territory of this group was in Offaly and Tipperary. During the Anglo-Norman invasion their influence became confined to that portion of Eile which later became known as Ely O Carroll; O Carroll of Loch Lein, near Killarney, who were dispossessed by the O Donoghues; O Carroll of Ossory who were descended from Cearball, a well known leader in the 9th century. The motto is "Strong in faith and war." Other meanings for this name, given by writers unacquainted with ancient and middle Gaelic, are without foundation.

> Cearḃ, *m.,* hart, stag
> Lat. *cervus.*

mac caisín, *mac Caissíg.*

McCashin, McKasshine, McCassin, MacCashin, Casheen, Cashin, Cashen, Cashion, Cassin, Keshin. The name is from the diminutive form of the Gaelic word *cas,* (curly, spiral or winding) and is therefore translated *descendant of a curly headed person.* The MacCashins were ancient hereditary physicians in Munster and Leinster. The Latin motto is translated: "The fields of our ancestors delight."

> Cap, *gsf.* caire, *a.,* crooked, curly, spiral, winding; wreathed, entwined, twisted

Mac Catmaoil Mac Caiτṁaoil.

McCaughwell, McCawill, McKavill, MacCavill, MacCawell, MacCowell, MacCowhill, MacCawl, MacCaul, MacCall, MacHall, MacCaulfield, Keawell, Howell, Caulfield. The root name is formed from the two Gaelic words *cath,* meaning battle and *maol* which from its meaning (bald, shaven, tonsured, etc.) came to mean also a religious devotee and, later, a devotee or follower in the lay sense. In this sense it is used here. Therefore Mac Cath Maoil is translated *son of the follower of battles.* According to O Donovan the descent is derived from Niall of the Nine Hostages. The family was powerful in Tyrone where they held the site of the present barony of Clogher up to the 16th century when they became scattered thruout Ireland. The word *maol* used here is not to be confused with a similar word meaning "chief" which comes from the ancient continental Celtic *melaglos.*

Caiṫ-eaġaρ, *m.,* a company in order of battle;

Ó Caoṁáin, Ó Caoṁáin.

O Keavane, O Kevane, Kevane, Keevane, Cavan, Kevans, Cavendish. The root name is from the Gaelic *caoiveaion,* (a gentle person). The family was of the Ui Fiachrach in Sligo and Mayo. It was their privilege to inaugurate the O Dowds as chieftains of the clan. In the 16th century this family also was dispersed thruout Ireland. Ó Caoṁánaiġ, Ó Caoṁánaiġ

Cavanagh, Kavanagh, Keaveny, Kevany, Kevans, Kevane. This is a more modern variant of the root name of O Kevane. The name was anciently interchangeable. The motto is "True valor relies on its own arms."

Caoṁán, -áin, *pl id., m.,* a gentle person; caoṁóg, *id.*

Ó Caisiḋe, Ó Caisiḋe.

O Cashedy, O Cassidy, Cassidy, Kassidy, Cassedy. The root name has the same origin and meaning as the root name of MacCashin. The family were hereditary physicians to the Maguires of Fermanagh. The motto is "Brave and faithful."

Caρ, -a, -anna, *m.,* a fold, a plait, curl.

mac ꝼlanncada,

mac ꝼlanҕcáꝺa.

MacClanchy, MacClanaghy, MacClanachy, Mac-Clanky, MacClansy, MacClancy, Clanchy, Clancy. The name is a form of the Gaelic *flann,* (ruddy). In the 12th century the family were hereditary brehons to the O Briens and resided at Knockfin and Cahermaclancy in Clare. The name originated in the 9th century.

ꝼlann-ꝺuinneaċ, ꝼ., bloody

O cléireacáin, O cléircín

O Cléꝑꝛeáċaꝑꝩ, O Cléꝑꝑiċꝩ.

O Clearkane, O Clercan, Clerihan, Clerkan, Clerkin, Clarkins, Clarke. The diminutive form of the word *cleireach,* (a cleric or clerk). There were two principal branches of this family; O Clerihan of Ui Cairbre Aevna, now represented by the Clerihans of Limerick and Tipperary; O Clerihan of Coillte Fallamhain in Meath, now represented by the Clerihans of Monaghan and Cavan.

O cléiriҕ, *O Cléꝑꝑuҕ.*

O Clery, O Cleary, Clery, Cleary, from the Gaelic *cleiriach,* (a clerk). This family name was originated by a descendant of Guaire, king of Connaught. They were early a literary family being poets and historians to the O Neills and O Donnells. The O Clerys of Tirconnell were the compilers of The Annals of the Four Masters. The O Clerys of Ulster later adopted the name "Clarke."

cléiꝑeaċ, -ꝛiҕ, *pl. id., dpl.* -ꝛċiꝺ, *m.,* a cleric, a clerk, an accountant.

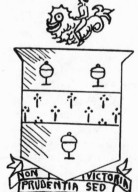

O coḃtaiҕ, *Ō Coḃċaꝩҕ.*

O Coffie, O Cohey, Coffey, Cowhey, Cowey, Cowhig. This name is from the Gaelic *covhach,* (creditor). The name originated in the 10th century. The following are its most distinguished families: O Coffey of Dunocowhey in Cork; O Coffey of Clonmacnowen in Galway; O Coffey of Umhall in Mayo; O Coffey of Westmeath; O Coffey of Derry. The family motto is "Not by prudence but by victory."

coḃċaċ, *m.,* a creditor

ṁac coʒáin, Ṁac Coʒáṝ.

McCogane, MacCogan, MacGoggan, Cogan, Coggan, Coogan. The root name is from the Gaelic *cogagh*, (aggression, strife, contention). The name originated in the 11th century with the chiefs of Clann Fearnaighe (anglicized Glanfarne) whose territory was in County Leitrim near Loch Allen. A branch of the family later settled in Meath. The Gaelic motto is translated "The red hand of Eire."

coʒaᵭ, *g.* -aiú, *pl.* -aiᵭe and -ʒᵵa, *m.*, war, battle; contention, strife

ṁac uallacáin, Ṁac Uallacáṝ

McCaulaghan, M'Wolleghan, Coulahan, Caulihan, Colahan, Coolahan, Colaghan. The name means "son of the proud" from the Gaelic *uallach*, (proud or haughty). The founders of the family were chiefs of Siol Anmchadha before the 11th century. In later centuries they were located at Lusmagh in Offaly. (See O Donovan's Ui Maine.)

uallaċ, -aiġe, *a.*, haughty, vain, boastful

ṁac ʒiolla comʒaill

Ṁac Ʒiolla Coiṁʒaṫl.

McGillachomhaill, McGillacoell, M'Gilleghole, McGillecole, McCole, MacCool, Gilhool, Cole. From the Gaelic *giolla*, (a guide or servant) and *Comghall*, (the personal name of an early Irish saint). The name may therefore be translated "son of a devotee of St. Cole." It has been prevalent in Donegal for many centuries. The motto is "Obey God and serve the king."

ʒiollaim, -aċt, -aiᵭeaċt, *v. tr.*, I lead, guide,

cóṁʒabáil, -ála, *f.*, bringing together; jointing; harmony, love, generosity.

o colmáin, Ō Colmáṝ.

O Colman, O Collomayne, Colman, Coleman. The root name is from the diminutive form of the Gaelic word *colm*, (a dove). It is therefore translated *descended from the little dove*. The family was a branch of the Ui Fiachrach and was seated in Templeboy, County Sligo up to the 16th century when it spread thruout eastern and southern Ireland. The name of a widely venerated Irish saint, Colmkille, is from this root word with the addition of the genitive form of the Gaelic *coill*, (a church).

colmán, -áin, dove

mac COLZAN   O COLZAN

Mac Colzaz.   *O Colzaz.*

McCollgan, MacColgan, Colgan, Collaghan, Colligan, Culligan, Quilligan. The root name is from the Gaelic *colgach*, (bearded or bristling). This was the name of a sept of the Oirghialla who were chiefs of Tirkeevan in Derry until dispossessed by the Cinel Eoghain, when they became erenaghs of Inishowen. A Thomond family of this name substituted the O for Mac.

Colzać, -aiże, *a.*, bearded, pointed, prickly

O COILeáin, *O Copleary.*

O Collaine, O Collan, Collan, Collins. This is from the Gaelic *coilleain*, (young hound). The family originated in the territory of the present County of Limerick where they were rulers of the present baronies of Upper and Lower Connello intermittently from the 9th to the 12th century. In 1178 they were subdued by invaders and the majority of them settled in West Cork. The remaining members retained power in Claonglass until about the beginning of the 14th century when their power passed to the Fitzgeralds. The motto is "Virtue conquers dangers."

Coileán, -áin, *pl. id.*, *m.*, a whelp, a puppy, a young dog; c. uapal, an enchanted whelp

mac CUMASCAIZ

Mac Cumapcaiz.

MacCumisky, MacCumesky, MacComiskey, Cumisky, Cumesky, Comisky, Cumeskey, Cumisk, (Comerford). The root name is from the Gaelic *cumasach*, (capable, powerful, vigorous). This surname had its origin in the clans of ancient Westmeath. The Annals show that the name was rarely found outside the boundaries of the territory comprising the present counties of Longford, Westmeath and Cavan. The Gaelic motto means "According to the wills of the gods."

Cumapać, -aiże, *a.*, capable, strong, powerful; vigorous

Ó connacτaiʒ, *Ó Coṁṗṡacaṡ*.

Connaty, Conaty, Connaghty, Conaghty, O Connaghty. This is from the Gaelic *Connaghtach* meaning "a native of the province of Connaught." The name originated in the 11th century and is recorded as that of a Breiffney family. It is still common in Cavan. The Gaelic motto means "Strike to help victory" or "Strike for victory."

Ó connacτáin, *Ó Coṁṗṡacaṡ*.

Connerton, Connorton, Connaghtane, Connaughton, Connaghtane, O Connaghtane. The root name is from the Gaelic *Connaghteen* a diminutive form of *Connaghtach,* (little Connaghtman) originating in the 11th century with a division of the Ui Fiachrach which once occupied the district of Cabragh in Sligo, scattered thru Limerick, Clare, Roscommon, Kerry and Donegal during the turmoil of the 16th century.

Connacτaċ, -aiʒ, *m.,* a native of Connaught ; *a.,* Connacian.

Ó conalláin, *Ó Coṁallaṡ*.

O Connellane, O Conlan, Connellan, Conlan. The name is from the Gaelic *connall,* (a sprout, stipule or stalk). Being in the diminutive form it may be translated *from the little sprout* and probably originated with a term of affection. The surname came into use in Roscommon as early as the 12th century.

Connall, -aill, *m.,* a stalk, a stipule, *whence* connlaċ,

Ó conbuiɒe, *Ó Coṁbuiɒe*.

O Connowe, Conboy, Conaboy, Conwy, Conee, Cunnoo, Conway. This name is from the two Gaelic words *con,* (hound or hunting dog) and *bwee,* (yellow). The surname came into use in the 9th century and was used by the following families. (1) O Conway of Tirergh in Sligo. (2) O Conway of Ui Maine, Galway. (3) O Conway of Dal Cas in Clare. The name became general in western Ireland in the 16th century. There were several forms of the original Gaelic name and the Mac replaced the O in Leinster and Munster. The Latin motto reads "By faith and love." Cú, *g.* con, *d.* coin, *pl.* cona, cuin, coin, coinτe, cuiτe, *f.,* a dog, a hound, a greyhound ; a hunting dog ; a hero

Ó CORBáin·

Ó Corbáıʒ.

O Corbane, O Coribane, Carbane, Corbett, Corbitt, Corbin. The root name is from the Gaelic verb *corbaim* meaning *I waste or destroy.* It originated in the clans of Munster in the 9th century. The Latin motto translated "God feeds the ravens," an expression of trust in Providence.

Corbaim, -aó, *v. tr.*, I waste, consume, torture, destroy.

Ó maolconaire, Ó maolcoyaʒʒ
Ó conaire·, Ó Coyaʒʒe.

O Mulchonery, O Mulconry, Mulconry, Conroy, Conry, Connery. The root name is formed from the two Gaelic words *maol,* (bald or shaven) but by use has also come to mean *follower or servant* and *connair,* (road or journey). It may therefore be translated *descended from one devoted to journeying, or a traveller.* The O Mulconry was a literary family, hereditary poets and chroniclers to the Kings of Connaught. They held territory in Roscommon by right of their profession. The name originated early in the 10th century. It was anciently associated with the poetry, chronicles and literature of Eire and was borne by many literary men even to comparatively recent times. The Gaelic motto is translated: "The strong hand uppermost."

Conaın, -e, *pl. id., f.,* a road, path; a journey.

Ó congalaıʒ, Ó Conʒalaʒʒ.

O Connally, O Connolly, O Conely, Connelly, Connally. The root name is derived from the Gaelic *congal,* (conflict). The surname was first used in the 10th century by a branch of the southern Ui Neill which possessed part of east Meath up to the Anglo-Norman invasion after which they became affiliated with the MacMahons of Monaghan. The surname was also that of: (a) a Dalcassian family of Thomond, descended from Mahon, brother of Brian Boru, (b) a Galway family of O Madden stock. The Latin motto is translated "Not for himself."

Conʒaıl, -e, *f.,* conflict.

Ó CONARÁIN ,

Ó Coṡaṗáṫ.

O Conoran, O Coneran, Conran, Condrin, Condron. The root name means "descendant of the little traveller" (see Connery). The name was that of the leaders of a sept in Offaly in the 9th century. The Annals show that it became scattered throughout Leinster at a comparatively early period.

Ó CUANA , *Ó Cuaṡ.*

O Cooney, Cooney, Cowney, Cunnea. The root name is from the Gaelic word *cuannacht,* (grace or elegance). According to the records the surname was founded by chiefs of Clan Fergus in Ulster in the 11th century. Before the end of the 16th century it had spread thruout Eire. It is now prevalent in Sligo, Cork and Kerry.

Cuannáċt, -a, *f.,* elegance. grace.

COIPINGÉIR , *Coppiṗṡéṗṡ.*

Copinger, Coppinger. From the Norse nickname *Kaupungr.* This surname was adopted by a Norse family which scattered in Cork in the 10th century, founded a clan after the Irish fashion and became prominent in Cork City where the family furnished mayors in the years 1319 and 1535. Their clan was attainted for rebellion in 1642 and 1691 because of their support of the Stuart cause.

Ó CORCRÁIN , *Ó Coṗcṗáṫ.*

O Corcrane, O Corkerane, O Corkran, Corcoran, Corkeran, Corkran. This name is from the diminutive form of the Gaelic word *corcar,* (purple). It is therefore translated *descended from the little purple one.* It was founded early in the 8th century by a family of hereditary *coarbs* or trustees of church estates which later became an ecclesiastical and literary family and, in this capacity, spread throughout Eire. The variations of this name are as follows: *O Corcra* which is anglicized Corkery and Corkerry and *O Corcain* which is anglicized O Corkan, Corken and Corkin. The Latin motto reads "Strong in faith and war."

Coṗcáṗ, -aiṗe and -cṗa, *pl.* -cṗa, *f.,* purple

Ó comראιοε,

Ō Coṁṗáιṭe.

O Cowrie, O Cory, O Curry, Corey and Curry. The root name is from the Gaelic word co(m)-rai(dg)e, (an affable person). The name became established in the 10th century and was the surname of the following families: (a) O Curry of Dal g Cais, a Thomond family to which belonged the illustrious Eugene O Curry; (b) O Curry of Westmeath who were chiefs of Ui MacUais; (c) O Curry of Cork, chiefs of Corca Laoighdhe. The motto is "I always aspire." The following are the variants of this name: O Corra which was anglicized O Corry, O Corr, Corra, Corr. O Corradhain which became O Curridane, O Corridan, Corridan and Cordan. O Corraidhe which became O Corrie, O Corry, Corree and Corry.

Cóṁṗáιṫċeaċ, -τιġe, a., affable; talkative; sm. an affable person, a conversationalist

Ó corraġáιn, Ō Coṁṗaġáṁṁ.

O Corrigane, O Currigan, Corrigan, Currigan, Corragan. The root name is the diminutive form of the Gaelic word Corr, (spear). The name is of 9th century origin and widely prevalent in Ulster, Leinster and Connaught. The Latin motto is translated "By wisdom and bravery."

coṁṁ-ġéaṁ, sharp-pointed

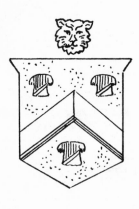

Ó coscraιġ, Ō Coṁċṗaṁ,

Ó coscraċáιn, Ō Coṁċṗaṁċáṁṁ.

O Coskery, O Cosgra, Coskery, Cosgry, Coskerry, Cuskery, Cosgriff, Cosgrive, Cosgreave, Cosgrave, Cosgrove. The root name is from the Gaelic coscroch, (fond of slaughter or carnage) or (destructively exultant). Originating with the lords of Feara Cualann in Wicklow in the 11th century this name came to signify also a Monaghan family, chiefs of Feara Rois, and a Galway family of the Ui Maine clans and affiliated with the O Madden. Variants of this name are: O Coscrachain, anglicized Coskeran, Cuskern; O Coscair, anglicized O Cosker, O Coskirr, Coscor, Cosker, Cusker.

coṁċṗaċ, -aιġe, a., carnage; al. coṁċaṁċaċ.

Mac Oisoealbaig Mac Coisceálbaig

Mac Oᵽoealbaᵹ, Mac Coᵽtealbaᵹ.

McCosdalowe, McCostelloe, McCostalaighe, Costelloe, Costello, Costellow, Costily, Costley. The root name is composed from the two Gaelic words *os,* (a deer or fawn) also (Os a nature god in Celtic mythology) and *dealv,* (shape or countenance). The translation is therefore "descended from the os-shaped or fawn-like." It is found in The Annals as early as A.D. 1193. The motto is "Do not seek thyself outside thyself." A variant of the original name *MacCoisdealv* is also anglicized Costello.

> Oᵽ, *g.* oiᵽ and uiᵽ, *pl. id.,* and oᵽᴀ, *m.,* a deer, a fawn: *dims.* oiᵽín, oᵽán.
> ᴅeᴀlbᴀᴅ, -bᴄᴀ, *m.,* act of shaping, forming, framing, warping.

Mac Oiᴄiᴚ, *Mac Oᵽᵽᵽ.*

McCotter, McCottir, M'Cottyr, MacCottier, MacCotter, Cotter, Otterson. The root name was originally the old Norse personal name *Ottar.* The family was of Norse origin from the Viking invasions. It was founded near Cork City in the 10th century. Some of its members later migrated to Ulster. The Latin motto is translated "While I live I hope."

Ó Coᴄláin, *Ó Coᴄláᵽᵹ.*

O Coghlane, O Coghlaine, Coghlan, Coughlin, Coglin, Coughlan. The root is the diminutive form of the Gaelic *cochall,* (a hooded cloak). It is therefore translated "descended from him of the little hooded cloak." It first appeared in Cork in the 11th century. It is prevalent in southern Ireland.

> Coᴄᴀll, -ᴀill, *pl. id., m.,* a cloak, a hood, any hood-like feature or object.

Ó Cuanᴀcáin, *Ó Cuaᵹᴀᴄáᵽᵹ*

O Coonaghan, Coonaghan, Counihan, Coonihan. From the Gaelic *cuanaght,* (grace or elegance). A variant of the Gaelic name which is anglicized Cooney and of the same Ultonian origin in clan Fergus but later established in Kerry.

Ó CUIRNÍN, Ó Cuirnín.

O Corneen, O Curneene, Curnin, Courneen, Courtney, O Kurnane, Curnane, Cournane. The root name is from the diminutive form of the Gaelic word *curn,* (a horn drinking cup). The name originated in the 12th century with a literary family who were poets and chroniclers to the O Rourkes of Breiffney. The motto is "Where have I been? What have I done?"

> Corn, g. cuirn, pl. id. corna and cóir-neaċa, m., a goblet, chalice, cup, drinking-horn, a horn (instrument)

Mac an Coiliġ, Mac an Coiliġ.

M'Ackolly, M'Anchelly, MacQuilly, translated Cox, Coxe. From the Gaelic *coileach,* (a male-bird). The surname was founded in the 10th century by a Roscommon family who were hereditary coarbs or stewards of the church lands of St. Barry at Kinbarry. A variant of this name, *Mac Concoille* which is anglicized MacEnkelly and MacInchelly, is found in Wickow and Tyrone. The motto is "By faith and fortitude." The name is not to be confused with another similar root name *concoille,* (hound of the woods).

> Coileaċ, -liġ, pl. id., m., a cock, a male bird

Ó Cadáin, Ó Cadáin.

O Coyne, O Kine, Coyne, Kine, Kyne, sometimes translated correctly *Barnacle*. The root name is from the Gaelic word *cai(d)han* meaning "the (wild) barnacle goose." The name was founded by a 12th century family of Connaught where it still prevails.

> Cadán, -áin, pl. id., m., a wild goose, a barnacle-goose; dim. caḋnóg.

Ó CORRAIDÍN, Ó Corraidín.

O Corrin, O Corren, O Currine, O Curran, O Currane, O Carran, O Corhane, Curran, Corran, Crain, Crane, Creane, Crean, Crahan, Crehan, Creen, Creaghan, Curreen. The root name and its derivatives are from the Gaelic *corrai(gh)eact,* (excessive or abundant). The name was founded in Munster in the 9th century.

> Corraiḋeaċt, -a, f., excess

Mac Oubsaill,

Mac Dubjajll.

McCool, McCaul, McCoole, McCole, McDoell, McDool, McDowell, McDowall, McDugal, McDougall, McDugald, MacDole, Doole, Dowell, Dugall, Dugald. The root name is from the two Gaelic words *dhuv,* (black) and *gall,* (foreigner). "Dhuvgall" was one of the names by which the Norse invaders came to be known in Eire before their defeat at Clontarf by Brian Boru in 1014 after which their survivors were assimilated into the native population. The name is therefore translated *son of the dark foreigner.* It belonged properly to a Scot-Irish family (kin to the McDonalds) and founded by So(m)airle, thane of Argyle who was slain in 1163. The MacDugalds and MacDonalds came to Ireland as captains of gallowglasses in the 14th century. They settled in northwest Eire and later spread into other parts of the country.

> Oub *a.,* dark
> Sallba, *a.,* foreign, strange,

O Cruaolaoic, *O Cruaslaojc.*

O Crowley, O Crowly, O Croley, O Croly, Crowley, Crawley, Croly, Crolly. The name is from the two Gaelic words *cruag,* (hard, firm, tough) and *laoch,* (a hero). According to MacFibris the name originated with Diarmaid an Cruaglaoch who was fourth in descent from Diarmaid the eponymous ancestor of the MacDermotts. The family was originally a branch of the MacDermotts of Roscommon whence they later migrated to Munster thruout which they are today known under the names Crowley and Crawley. The motto is: "Always faithful to my friends." Cruabaim. -bab, *v. tr.* and *intr.,* I harden

> Laocmar, -air, *m.,* heroism, valour.

AMICIS FIDELIS. SEMPER

O Croioeagáin, *O Crojoeazájy.*

O Cridigan, O Crigane, O Crigan, Creeghan, Creigan, Cregan, Creggan, O Criane, Cree, Creddon. The root name and its variants are from the diminutive form of the Gaelic *croi(dh)e,* "heart" (even now used as a term of endearment). The name was assumed by a family which formed part of the Cinel Eoghain in Sligo, in the 15th century. The Latin motto is translated "Create in me a clean heart O my God."

> Croibe, *g. id., pl.* -óce; -beabá, -bceacá and cra(ó)ćacá, *m.,* the heart; love, affection; the centre or core

COR MUNDUM DEUS. CREA IN ME,

Ó CRAOIUE,

Ó Craoybe.

O Crevy, Creevy, Creevey, O Crevan, Creaven, Creavin. The root name and its variants are from the Gaelic *craoiveach*, (branching or branchy). In this sense, "prolific." The family was founded in Sligo in the early part of the 8th century. It is mentioned in The Annals as being an affiliation of the Cinel Eoghain in A. D. 760. The motto is "Faithful to the end."

> Cṛaoḃ, *q.* -oiḃe and -oḃa, *d.* -oiḃ. *pl.* -ḃa and -ḃaċa, *f.*, a branch, a bough,

CRAOUAĊ, *Craoḃaċ.*

Creagh, Creavagh, Cray. The name is from the Gaelic *craov*, meaning a branch. The family was founded by one of the early O Neills of Clare who carried a green branch as a family emblem in a battle with the Danes at Limerick in the beginning of the 11th century.

> Cṛaoḃaċ, -aiġe, *a.*, branching, full of boughs

Ó CRIOĊÁIn, *Ó Cṛiocáỳ.*

O Criaghan, O Creghan, Crehan, Creighton, Creaton. The root name is from the diminutive form of the Gaelic *creach*, meaning a raider, spoiler or plunderer. The records indicate that this surname originated with a 10th century Oriel family seated in Tyrone. The name was scattered thru Eire before the 17th century.

> Cṛeaċ, *g.* cṛeice, *pl.* cṛeaċa, *f.*, plunder, spoil, booty, cattleprey; plundering expedition, a raid

mac COnĊRuaĊan,

mac ConCṛuaċaỳ.

MacEncroghan, M'Necroghan, Croughan, Croghan, Crohan, Croan. This name is from the Gaelic words *cu*, (a hound) and *cruachain*, (a little hill). It is therefore translated *descended from the hound or guardian of the little hill or mound*. It has been a Roscommon surname from early times. It is recorded in The Annals under date of the 8th century.

> Cṛuaċán, -áin, *pl. id.*, *m.*, a little hill

mac an CROSÁIN, *Mac an Grosáin.*

M'Ancrossane, McEcrossan, MacCrossan, Crossan, Crossin, Cross, Crosbie, Crosby. The root name is from the Gaelic *crossawn,* (a rhymer or crooner). It was founded by a Tirconnell family in the 12th century. Their descendants are still numerous in Derry and Tyrone. Members of this family were also bards and poets to the O Moores and O Connors of Leix and Offaly. The family accepted the English in the 16th century and generally assumed the anglicized name form of "Crosbie." The motto is "Spurning enemy: the just shall flourish." cpónán, -áin, *m.*; Croon,

cpopánaċt, -a, *f.*, a sort of versification.

ó cuioiżtiż, *Ó Cuddyżys.*

O Codihie, O Kuddyhy, O Cuddie, Cuddihy, Cudihy, Cuddehy, Quiddihy, Cuddy, Cody. The root name is from the Gaelic *cuidigheach,* (helper, helping or assisting). The family name originated in the 9th century. It later became an important Ormond surname. The motto is "Lift up thy heart."

Cuioeaċtain, -ana, *f.* act of helping, taking part with; company, society

ó cuimin, *Ó Cummyn.*
ó comáin, *Ó Commayn.*

O Comane, O Comman, O Cowmane, Coman, Commane, Cowman, Cummane, Commons. The root name is from the Gaelic *camaan,* (bent or curved) especially a curved stick used in playing the national game of hurling. The name is therefore translated *descended from the hurler.* A variant of this name O Curmeen, is anglicized O Cumyn, Cumin, Cummin, Cummins, Cummings. The name was originally that of a Sligo family of the Ui Fiachrach as indicated by the records of the 13th century. It is now found in all the provinces but more especially in Munster.

Caman, -ain, *pl. id., m.,* a bend; a stick with a crooked head; a hurley fo ball-playing;

mac coluim, *Mac Coluym*

MacColum, MacCollum, MacCollom, Collum, Colum. This has its foundation in the Gaelic *colm,* (a dove). In Gaelic it is also a synonym for tenderness. It is of early origin in Antrim whence it was carried with the Gaels to Scotland where it has been anglicized MacCallum.

Colm, *g.* cuilm, *pl. id.,* and colma, *m.,* a dove; *al.* a pigeon; C. Cille, *lit.* Dove of the Church, Columcille:

mac cumascais

mac Cumascais.

MacCumisky, MacCumesky, MacComiskey, Cumisky, Cumesky, Cumiskey, Comesky, Comiskey, Commiskey, Cumisk, Comerford, Cummerford. The name is from the Gaelic *cumasach*, (capable or vigorous man). It was founded before the 13th century and in Eire it is almost peculiar to Cavan, Westmeath and Longford.

> Cumar, -air, *old g.* requisite capability or power; ability;

mac cruitin, *mac Cruitin.*

McCrutten, McCruttan, MacCurtain, Curtin, Curtis, Curtayne, Curtain. The root name is the Gaelic *cruiteen,* (hunch backed). The family is of 11th century origin in Clare where their territory constituted the lands fo Carrowduff (black quarter) in the parishes of Killasbuglonane and Lavally. They were Annalists and Chroniclers to the rulers of Thomond. Branches of this family settled in Limerick and Cork in the 16th century. In later times poets of this name contributed to Gaelic literature. The motto is: "To the brave and faithful nothing is difficult."

> Cruitin, *g. id., pl.* -i, *m.,* a hump on the back; a hunchback

mac toirdealbais,

mac Toirdealbais

M'Torrilogh, M'Turlogh, M'Terrelly, M'Tirlay, M'Terrens, Torley, Turley, Terrance, Terry, McCuryle, McKyrrelly, MacCorley, MacKerley, MacKerlie, MacGorley, Corley, Kerley, Kirley, Curley. The root name which was popular in the family and clan of Brian Boru is composed of the two words *Thor,* (the Jupiter of Scandinavian mythology) and the Gaelic *dealbach,* meaning shape or countenance. The name may be translated *son of him who resembles Thor.*

> -Dealbac, -aige, in *compds.* -form, -formed.

ó cuinneacáin, *Ó Cuinneacáin*

O Quinegane, Cunningan, Kinnegan, Kinnighan, O Kineghan, Ó Kynaghan, O Quenahan, Cunningham, Cunnahan, Cunihan, Kinaghan, Kinghan, Kinnighan, Kinnan, Keenan, Cunninghan. The root name is a diminutive form of the Gaelic *conn,* (sense or reason). An ancient and widely prevalent name. See Quinn.

> Conn, *g.* cuinn, *m.,* sense, reason

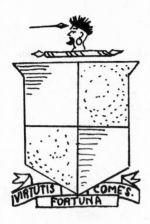

ᴠᴇ cíoṁsóᵹ, ᴠᴇ cíuṁsóᵹ,

de Cᵱoᵹᵱsóᵹ, de Cᵱuᵹᵱsóᵹ.

de Kisshok, deKeusaac, de Cusaak, de Cusack, Cusack, Cusick. This is from the Norman *de Cusak* i.e. of Cussac in France. This family came with the Anglo-Norman judiciary and in this capacity they functioned importantly in Norman Irish territory. In common with the Gael they espoused the Stuart cause and were attained and dispersed during and after the Jacobite war which culminated in the treaty of Limerick in 1691. The name is now prevalent in Munster. The motto is "Fortune is the compensation of virtue."

ᴏ ᴅáᴌᴀıᵹ, Ō ᴅáᴌᴀᵹᴊ.

O Daly, Daly, Dawley, Daley. This is from the Gaelic *dailach* meaning, frequenting or given to holding assemblies. The name was founded by a scion of Maine, son of Niall of the Nine Hostages. The family originally headed Corca Adain in the present Westmeath in the 9th century. Later they became hereditary bards, teachers and chroniclers. According to O Donovan their contributions to ancient Gaelic learning and literature are unexcelled by any other ancient literary family. Cuchonnacht O Daly who died at Clonard in 1139 was known as *Cuchonnact na Sgoile* (of the schools) because of the many institutions of learning which he fostered. Later Donogh More O Daly, bard to the O Loghlens of Burren in Clare founded a family which, migrating to Galway in the 15th century, became judges to the O Kellys of Ui Maine. Another branch of the family, founded by Ragnaill O Daly, settled in Desmond where they became ollaves to clan McCarthy. Other branches became poets to the O Reillys of Cavan, to the O Neills of Ulster and to the O Connors of Connaught. The name is now prevalent in all Eire. The motto is "Faithful to my God and my king."

ᴅáᴌᴀċ, *a.*, of meetings; given to holding meetings.

ᴏ ᴅᴇᴀᵹᴀın-, Ō ᴅᴇᴀᵹᴀᵹᴊ.

O Dyeane, O Deane, O Dane, Dean, Deane, Deen, Dane. This is from the Gaelic *dea(gh)an* meaning a foster father. This name had its origin in southern Ireland in the 14th century. The motto is "To the brave and faithful nothing is difficult."

ᴅᴇᴀᵹᴀn, -ᴀın, *m.*, a dean; a tutor, a foster father

Ó ꝺáiṁín, Ó Daiṁíġ.

O Davine, O Dovine, O Devine, Davine, Devine, Davin, Deven, Devon, Devins. The name is from the diminutive form of the Gaelic *dhaiv,* (a poet). It came into use with a branch of the Oriel who were of the sept Maguire and were chiefs of Tirkennedy in Fermanagh. Today it is anglicized Devine in Ulster and Davin in Munster and sometimes Davy in Connaught.

ꝺáiṁ, poetic

Ó ꝺoꝛcaiꝺe, Ó ꝺoꝛcaiꝺe

O Doroghie, O Dorghie, O Dorchie, Dorcey, Darkey, Darcy, Dockery. The root of this name is the Gaelic *dorcach* meaning a dark person. The name originated in a branch of the Ui Fiachrach in Mayo. Their territory was in Partry, west of Lough Mask. Another family of this name belonged to the Ui Maine in Galway. Before the end of the 16th century the name became widespread in southern Ireland. The French motto is translated "One God, one king." The anglicization D'Arcy disguises the Gaelic origin of this name.   D'Arcy, Darcy, from the Norman de Arcy, that is from Arci in Normandy. These were consequential leaders of the Normans who, after residing in England for some centuries, branched into Ireland. ꝺoꝛcact, -a, ꝼ, darkness, blackness; eclipse; mysteriousness; al. ꝺoiꝛceact

mac ꝺaꝛa,

mac ꝺaꝛa.

MacDara, Daragh, Darragh, Darrogh, Oak, Oakes, Darrock. The original name is from a derivative of the Gaelic word *dhair,* (an oak tree). The family heraldic motto is "In this sign conquer." ꝺaꝛac, -aiġe, a., oaken, firm as an oak; a place abounding in oaks

Ó ꝺaꝟoiꝛeann, Ó ꝺaꝟoꝛꝛeaġġ.

O Davoren, O Daverin, O Davern, Davoran, Davoren, Davern. The root name is from the Gaelic *dhavair* which in ancient Gaelic meant a stream and in modern Gaelic means a downpour. It is therefore translated *descended from him of the streams, or a riverman.* The name originated in the 9th century with a hereditary brehon family of Clare, seated at Corcomroe where for many generations they conducted a legal school which was once attended by MacFibris, the antiquary who is frequently quoted in these pages. The leader of the sept was resident of Lisdoonvarna. The motto is "Never unprepared."

ꝺaꝟaiꝛ, ꝼ., a downpour

Ó ᴅEᴀᴅᴀıᴢ, ó ᴅeᴀᴅᴀʒʒ.

O Deadie, Deady, Dady. From the Gaelic *daedh*, (a tooth). Therefore it is translated *of the (prominent) teeth*. This is a rare Munster surname which found mention in records dating back to the 13th century.

> ᴅéᴀᴅ, -éıᴅ, *pl. id.*, *m.*, the teeth, a set of teeth, tusks; *smt.* a tusk

Ó ᴅuıᴃᴢeᴀnnᴀın, Ó ᴅuıʒınn,

O Duigenain, Duigenan, Duignam, Dignan, Deignan, Duignan, Dignam, Digin, Diggin, Deegin, Digan, Deegan, Duigan, Dugan, Duggan. A diminutive compound of the Gaelic *dhuv*, (black) and *ceann*, (head). The name was first assumed in the 11th century by a family of Roscommon who became chroniclers to the septs of MacDermotts, O Farrells and MacGrannells. Branches of this family later settled in Clare, Wexford, Galway, Leix and Offaly.

> ceᴀnn-ᴅuᴃ, *a.*, black-headed

mᴀc ᴀn ᴅéısıᴢ, mᴀc ᴀn ᴅéịʒʒ.

MacEdesey, Deacy, Deasey. From *Deisheach*, (a native of the Decies, southern territory, part of Waterford). A name assumed by an ancient Sligo family. The French motto is translated "Always ready."

> ᴅéıᴘeᴀᴄ, -ıʒe, *a.*, facing towards the south, southerly.
> ᴅéıᴘeᴀᴄ, -ıʒe, *a.*, of the Decies; *sm.*, a native of the Decies.

ᴅe ᴌeıs, ᴅe ᴌéịʒ.

De Lesse, de Lease, De Lacy, Dacy, Lacey. From the Norman de Laci, meaning *of Lassy,* in France. This family was founded by Hugh de Lacy who came to Ireland with the Anglo-Norman invaders. To a branch of this family in Limerick belonged Pierce Lacy of Bruff, a leader in the wars against Elizabeth. This Norman Irish family also produced many persons who became important in continental Europe, notably Count Peter de Lacy, born in Limerick in 1678, who became military commander of Russia and his son Maurice who was Marshall of the armies of Austria. A de Lacy of Limerick was a famous general and diplomat of 18th century Spain.

Ó DUBSLÁINE, Ó Dubisláinge.

O Dowlaney, O Dulany, Delaney, Delany, Deleaney, Laney, Staney. The name is from the Gaelic compound *dhuv-(s)lawn*, meaning challenge or defiance. It is therefore translated *descended from the challenger*. It is the name assumed by the 12th century chiefs Coill Uachtarach (Upperwoods) at the foot of Slieve Bloom. Because of the anglicized form this name has been erroneously classed as Norman Irish.

> Dub-ślán, -áin, *m.*, challenge, defiance; bravado, foolhardiness, the spirit of challenge

Ó DUINEACDA, Ó Duineacda.

O Denaghie, Dennahy, Dennehy, Dannahy, Danihy, Denehy, Denny. The root name is from the Gaelic *deuneachai(dh)*, meaning humane. An ancient Cork surname recorded in The Annals as early as the 11th century. The Latin motto reads "For our altars and our firesides."

> Duineatát, -a, *f.*, humanity, kindness

Ó DIARMADA, Ó Diarmada.

O Dermott, O Dermody, Dermody, Darmody, Dermott, Darby. Descended from Diarmaid, an ancient personal name which in old Gaelic meant freeman or common man, (the John Q. Public of those days). The Annals indicate that this surname has been in existence in all parts of Ireland since the 10th century.

Ó DEASMUMNAIŻ, Ó Deasmumnaiż.

O Dassuny, O Dasshowne, O Deason, O Desmonde, Desmond. From the Gaelic compound *deas*, (south) and *Mu(m)nac*, (a Munster man). A Cork surname of the 13th century.

> Dearmuma, g. -n, *f.*, South Munster, Desmond.
>
> Dearmuimneać, *a.*, belonging to Desmond; *sm.*, a Desmond man.

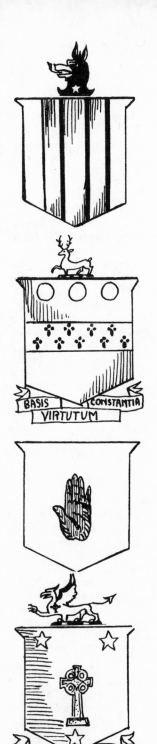

Ó ᵭubáin, Ó ᵭubáᵹᵹ.

O Doyane, O Dwane, O Duan, O Dowane, O Doane, O Downe, Dewane, Devane, Duane, Dune, Doane, Doon, Downes. The root name is from the Gaelic *dhuvawnaie*, (an angler, a fisherman). This is the name of several separate Gaelic families of which the following are the more important: (a) a Limerick family established in the 13th century. (b) a family of Corca Laoighe in southwest Cork. (c) a Connemara family founded in the 10th century and affiliated with the O Kellys of Ui Maine in the wars against the Danes. (d) a Meath family, once leaders of a sept in the district now called Knowth.

ᵭubánaióe, *g. id., pl.* -óᵼe, *m.,* an angler.

Ó ᵭubraic, Ó ᵭubᵼnᵼoᵼc.

O Duvrick, O Durick, O Dowricke, Durack, Durik, Darrick, Devery, O Divirick, Dever and sometimes Devereux. The root word is from the Gaelic *dhuvruach*, (successful). A Family of the Dal Cas founded at Ui Congaile (now O Connelloe) in Clare toward the end of the 10th century. It was attainted in Clare by the Cromwellians about 1642 but survived in Tipperary and Offaly. The motto is "Constancy is the foundation of virtue."

ᵭubᵼuaᵼ, success

Ó ᵭuibeannaiᵹ, Ó ᵭuᵼᵬesᵹᵹaᵼᵹ

O Doveanna, O Devenie, Devanny, Devaney, Devany, Devenny, Divney, Divenney. This is from the compound Gaelic word *dhuv-ean*, (a cormorant or diving sea bird). This is a County Down family which appears in the chronicles early in the 12th century. They later migrated to southern Ireland. A bishop of this family, Connor O Devany, is mentioned in The Annals of the Four Masters as having been martyred in Dublin in 1612.

ᵭuiᵬ-éan, *m.,* a cormorant.

Ó ᵭoᵭailein, Ó ᵭoᵬaᵼleᵼᵹ

O Devlin, Develin, Devlin, from the diminutive of the Gaelic *dhotail,* meaning one who daubs, plasters, a dauber. The name was assumed by the chiefs of Corca Firthri in Sligo in the 11th century. It is recorded in The Annals that it was also the surname of the chiefs of Muintir Devlin in Tyrone. The motto is "The Cross is my star."

ᵭóiᵬeaᵼl, -álᴀ, *f.,* act of plastering; daubing.

Ó Ouḃuiḋe, Ó Auḃuiḋe.

Devoy, Deevey, Deevy. The root name is from the old Gaelic *dhuvui(g)eact*, meaning melancholy. A very ancient surname in Leix and Offaly, mentioned in The Annals of the Danish wars of the 10th century.

Ouiḃeaċaḋ, *m.*, a darkening, overcasting

Oíolṁain, Oíolún, Ofolṁayy, Ofolúy.

Dillon, Dilloun, from the old Teutonic *Dilli* with the Norman-French suffix—*on*. A Norman-French family which came to Eire with the Anglo-Norman invasion. Sir Henry Dillon was granted territory in Westmeath by King John. This territory came to be known as Dillon's country after the family became affiliated with the native Gael. One branch of the family attained to the barony of Kilkenny West while another settled in Mayo. The Dillons, with many other Norman-Irish families, espoused the cause of the Stuarts in the Jacobite-Orange war. After the Treaty of Limerick they were attainted and outlawed. Many of them joined the other Irish exiles which formed the Irish Brigades in the Continental wars of the 18th century during which their leaders displayed notable military ability. The Latin motto reads "While I live I hope."

Ó Ouinnín, Ó Ouyyyy.

Dinneen, Dineen, Dunion, Denning, O Dunnyne, O Downie, Downing, Dunning, from the genetive form of the diminutive, of the Gaelic *dhonn,* (brown, brown-haired). Founded in the 10th century, the heads of this family became hereditary historians to the MacCarthy More. The name has assumed the forms Dunning and Denning in Northern Eire and Dinneen in the South.

Oonn, *gsf.* Ouinne or Ooinne, *a.*, brown, brown-haired

Ó Ouḃláin, Ó Auḃláyy.

O Dolane, O Dowlane, O Doolan, Doolan, Dolan, Dowlan, Dowlin, Doolen, Dowling, Doolin, from the Gaelic *dhuvslain,* (defiance). Originating as a branch of the O Kellys of Ui Maine in Galway (12th century) this family spread rapidly thruout the country. The name appears in many of the chronicles.

Ouḃrlán, *n.*, a challenge.

Ó Docartaiġ Ó Docaptaïġ.

O Dogherty, O Dougherty, Dougherty, Doherty, Doghartie. The root name is from the Gaelic *docararch,* (unfortunate). The family was originally a branch of Cinel Connaill of the root stock O Donnell. They were chiefs of Cinel Enna and Aodha Miodhair from which they advanced to control of Innishowen at the close of the 14th century. In the reign of James I their leader Sir Cahir O Dogherty rebelled, suffered defeat and was outlawed. His peoples' possessions were confiscated and they were dispersed. Later the name became widespread thruout Eire. Their Gaelic motto is translated "Army (and) Country."

Ⓓocàpaċ,' -aiġe, *a.,* unfortunate.

Ó Domnallàin, Ó Domgallary.

O Donlan, O Donnellane, O Donellane, Donelan, Donellan, Donlan, from the diminutive form of the compound Gaelic word *dhownall,* (world power). The principle family of the name is a 12th century branch of the O Kellys of Ui Maine. Its leaders were chiefs of clan Breasail near Ballinasloe and had residence at Ballydonnellan. At least two poets of this branch are referred to in the ancient chronicles. Another family of the name had its origin in the Orghialla and produced a sub-branch, a brehon family of Offaly. Most of the present Donnellans and Donlans are descended from the Ui Maine.

Ⓓoman, world, All, *a.,* great.

Ó Donnaġàin, Ó Domgagary.

Ⓓonn-, Ⓓoinn-, brown

O Donegan, O Dungan, O Dongan, O Donegaine, Dunegaine, Donegan, Dunegan, Dungan, Dongan, Duncan. The name is a diminutive form of the Gaelic *dhonn* (brown). In the 10th century there were three important clan-leading families of this name: (1) O Donegan of Ara (in Tipperary) and Ui Cuanach (Limerick) whose names are found connected with numerous important events recorded in The Annals of the 11th and 12th centuries. They were overcome by the Anglo-Norman invaders and their interests were later conveyed to a branch of the O Briens of Thomond under the clan of Mac Ui Brian Ara. (2) O Donegan of Cork, contemporaries of the aforementioned, who had possession of Muscraighe-tri-Maighe (Muskerry-three-Plains) which, as a conquered territory under King John, passed to Sir William de Barry under the name of Muskerry-Donnegan. (3) O Donegan of Ulster and North Connaught who, according to the 11th century Annals, were leaders of northern clans.

ó ᴏuɪnnsᴛeɪᴅe,

Ó Duᴜᴢᴢᴊᴛéɪᴅe.

ᴅonn, *g.* ᴏuɪnn, *m.,* a prince,
a chief.

sᴛɪᴀᴅ, -ᴛéɪᴅe, a mountain

O Donlevy, O Dunlevy, O Downlay, Dunlavy, Dunlevy Dunleevy, Dunleavy, Dunlea, Dullea, Delea, Delay, Delee, from the Gaelic and Spanish *dhon,* (a lord) and *sleive,* (of the mountain) therefore *descended from the lord of the mountain.* Sometimes known by the Gaelic form which has become Mac Dunlevy, they were of the root family O hEocadja of the clans of Ulster in the 9th century.

Their principal sphere of influence was in what is now County Down where, after some centuries of power, they were defeated by John De Courcy in a three day battle at Down Patrick in 1177. Subsequently their clans were dispersed and the leading family became hereditary physicians to the O Donnells. Others found new spheres of influence in northern Eire and in Scotland. Under the "Mac" prefix the root name took various other anglicized forms such as M'Anlevy, M'Enleive, M'Enlevie, M'Enleve, M'Colley, MacConloy, MacEnleavy, MacAleavy, MacAlea, Macleavy, MacClew, MacCloy, Killeavy, Leavy, MacInleavin, MacLevin, Lavin.

VIR SUPER HOSTEM

ó ᴏonnaᴍáɪn, *Ó Doᴢᴢanᴊáᴢᴢ.*

O Donovan, Donavan, Donavin, from the diminutive derivative of the Gaelic *dhonn,* (brown). A family of 9th century origin, chiefs of a sept of Corca Laoighdhe later led by the O Donovans of Cairbre. These were ancestors of all O Donovans of Cork and of the O Donovan Rossa. They are frequently mentioned in The Annals of the Four Masters. The motto is "A man above an enemy."

ᴅonnᴀɪm, -ᴀᴅ, *v. tr.* and *intr.,* I make brown; I get brown

VIRTUS IPSA NITITUR ARMIS
SUIS FIRMISSIMA

ó ᴏuᴅᴅᴀ, *Ó Dubᴅᴀ.*

O Dowd, O Doud, O Dowda, O Dooda, Dowdie, Doody, Duddy, Doud, Dowd, from a variant of the Gaelic *dhuv,* (black). The origin of the family was a descendant of King Dathi and was progenitor of the chiefs of the powerful clan of the Northern Ui Fiachrach which flourished in part of the present counties of Mayo and Sligo prior to the English invasion of Connaught in 1237. The motto is "Bravery is best sustained by arms."

ᴅuᴅ-ᵹnúɪᴘeᴀċ, *a.,* black-feced.

Ó Ouḃlaoiċ, Ó Ouḃlaoiċ.

O Dowley, O Dooley, Dowley, Dooley, Dooly, from the compound Gaelic word *dhuvlaoch*, meaning dark warrior. The O Dooleys were of the race of Feidlimidh son of Enna Cennseelach, and in the 9th, 10th and 11th centuries, were lords of Feara Tulagh (now Fertullagh) in the present County Westmeath. After the invasion their territory came into possession of the Tyrells. Another branch of this family was in control of Clann Mhaonaigh. According to MacFirbis they were banished from Meath in the 11th century and settled in Ely Carroll where they obtained the privilege of inaugurating the O Carroll kings of Ely. Laoċ, *g.* Laoiċ, *pl. id.* a champion, a warrior,

Ó Oeóráin, Ó Oeóráin.

O Dorian, O Doweraine, O Dowerine, O Dorrane, O Doran, Dorian, Dorrian, Doran, Dorran, from the Gaelic *dheora*, (alien or exile). This name is that of a great brehon family of Leinster in the 9th to 13th centuries. The motto is: "Hope is the anchor of life." Oeoṛa, -ò, *ds.* -iò, *pl.* -aí, *m.*, an alien,

Ó Oúnaoaiġ, Ó Oúnaoaiġ.

O Downie, O Downy, O Duny, O Dony, Dooney, Downey, Doney, Donney, Dunny, Dunning, from a derivative of the Gaelic *dhun*, meaning a fort or stronghold. The name is therefore translated *descended from the holder or owner of the stronghold*. It is of 9th century origin and pertained to several distinct families of which the following are the most important. O Downey of Luachair (Country of the Rushes) comprising sections of the present Cork, Kerry and Limerick. O Dooney of Siol Anmchadha in Galway, a branch of the O Maddens; O Downy of Corca Laoighdhe, Cork, a sept of the clan O Driscoll. The Gaelic motto reads "The strong hand uppermost." Oúnaȯeaċ, -oiġ, *m.*, a fortress-holder,

Ó Ouḃġaill, Ó Ouḃġaill.

O Dowilly, O Doyle, Doyle, Dowell, O Dowill, Doole. Another name which is a compound of the two Gaelic words *dhuv*, (black) and *gall*, (stranger, foreigner) i.e. "one descended from the dark stranger" a name anciently given to the Irish descendants of the Norse Vikings. The name is general thruout Eire but most prevalent in the maritime counties of Leinster and Munster, sites of the 8th century Viking strongholds in Eire.

Ouḃ-ġall, a Dane, a foreigner.

Ó Duinn, Ō Duinn.

O Dunne, O Doyne, Dunne, Dunn, Dun, Doyne, Dyne, from the Gaelic *dhonn,* (brown or brown-haired). The O Duinn ui Riagain (now Iregan) were chiefs of a sept of the Ui Failghe in Leinster as early as the 11th century. Their territory was co-extensive with the present barony of Tinnahinch in Leix. A related family was the O Duinn of Tara. The Gaelic motto is translated "Mullagh to victory."

donn-ḃallaċ, brown-spotted

Ó hEidirsceoil, Ō hEidirsceoil.

O Driscoll, Driscoll, O Driscole, O Hederscoll, O Hidirscoll, from a compound Gaelic word derived from *idhir,* (between, intervening) and *sgeal,* (a statement, a story). The name is therefore translated *descended from the interpreter.* Prior to the 12th century the O Driscolls were chiefs of clans in Carberry, Beare and Bantry. They were later partially supplanted by the O Donovans, O Mahonys and O Sullivans and their sphere of influence was limited to the maritime district around Baltimore. In this district they held several strong castles down to the 17th century. At the termination of the Elizabethian-Irish war in the Irish defeat at Kinsale the O Driscoll territory passed to Lord Castlehaven.

eadarġaba
intervene.

Ó Duḃagáin, Ō Duḃagáin.

O Dooghaine, O Dowgaine, O Doogan, Duggan, Dougan, Dugan, Duggan, Duggen, Doohan. Another derivative of the Gaelic *dhuv,* (black). There were several distinct families of this name of which the following are the more important. (1) O Doogan of Ballydugan, Galway, who were hereditary historians to the O Kellys of Ui Maine and were compilers of the Book of Ui Maine. (2) O Doogan of Cork, a sept of Corca Laoighdhe. (3) O Doogan of Mayo, affiliates of the sept MacFibris and seated near Ballina.

Duḃáinín, *g. id., m.,* a small black thing,

Ó Duḃtaiġ, Ō Duḃtaiġ.

O Duffie, O Duhie, O Duhig, O Downie, O Dowey, O Dully, Duffy, Dowey, from a derivative of the Gaelic *dhuv,* (black). Of 9th century Dalcassian origin this family became powerful as a church family in Connaught. The name later took the form Dowey and Dooey in Ulster; Duhug, and O Duffy in Munster.

Duḃta, *p. a.,* blackened, blighted

Ó Ɒuinnɔinn,

Ó Ɒuɲɲiɔɲɲ

O Dingine, O Dongyn, O Dongen, Dongen, Dinkin, Dunkin, Duncan, from the Gaelic *dhonn,* (brown) and *ceann,* (a head). A Sligo family of 9th century origin. The name is now frequently spelled Duncan. The Latin motto is translated "Brave and faithful."

> Ceᴀnn, *d. id.,* and cionn, *g.* cinn, *pl. id.* and ceᴀnnᴀ, *m.,*   a head

Mᴀc Ɒuᴀrᴄᴀ́in, *Mᴀc Ɒuᴀɲiᴄᴀɲɲ*

MacGurgan, Gurkin, Durcan, Durkan, Durkin, from the Gaelic *dhuarachain,* (a pessimist). Originating before the 11th century as a branch of the O Haras, this family attained to the leadership of Cuil Neiridh in Sligo.

> Ɒuᴀɲcᴀ́n, -ᴀ́in, *m.,* a pessimist, a gloomy or reticent person.

Ó Mᴀolmoᴄóir, *Ó Mᴀolɲ̇oᴄóɲɲ.*

O Mulmochore, O Mulmochory, O Molvochary, O Culluchrie, Early, Earley, Eardley, from a Gaelic compound word meaning *devoted to early rising.* This surname originated with hereditary coarbs of church property in Leitrim and Cavan, seated at Drumreilly and Drumlane, whence they spread as an ecclesiastical family in Roscommon, Sligo and Donegal.

> Moᴄóiɲ, -óɲᴀ, -ɲí, *m.,* an early-riser

Mᴀc ᴀoɒᴀᵹᴀ́in, *Mᴀc ᴀoɒᴀᵹᴀɲɲ.*

M'Egaine, M'Heagan, McKeagan, McKiegane, MacEgan, MacKeegan, Egan, Heagan, Keegan, from the diminutive form of the Gaelic *aodh* which anciently meant Fire or a Fire-god (Celtic mythology) and later came into use as a personal name translated modernly to Hugh. Originally a brehon family of the Ui Maine, this family migrated to southern Eire in the 14th century, becoming law givers to various chieftains. The Annals mention them as conducting many schools of law. The motto is "Fortitude and prudence."

> ᴀoɒ, -ᴀ, *m.,* a man's name; Hugh is often used as an Eng. equivalent; the word means fire; *dims.* ᴀoɒᴀiɒín ᵹ ᴀoɒᴀᴄᴀ́n.

easmonn, Eapmoqq.

Estmund, Eatmond, Esmund, Esmond, Esmonde. An Anglo-Saxon personal name it first appears as "Estmunt" in the Doomesday Book. In the Dublin Roll of Names, A.D. 1216, the founder of this Irish family is recorded as "Willielmus filius Estmundi." The family settled in Wexford where, in 1303, Henry Estmund provided ships for the transportation to Scotland of the Irish contingent of the army of Edward I. The motto is "Death rather than disgrace."

iústás   júpcáp.

Eustace. A common Norman French name which came to Ireland with the Norman-English invasion. The Norman-English Eustaces became established in Kildare and Carlow and soon were numbered with the powerful Norman-Irish families which opposed other English invaders. They allied themselves with the O Byrnes and O Tooles and in 1580 this alliance defeated the English army at Glenmalure. The failure of promised material help from the Spanish alliance rendered their efforts futile and the Eustaces became attainted and outlawed. Their leaders were hunted down and executed and all power passed from their hands before the end of the 17th century. The motto is "Glory to God alone."

Ó néimín,   O hEimín. O hEimeáng.

O Hevine, Evin, Evine, Evans, from the diminutive form of the Gaelic *eiv*, (swift, active). An 11th century Thomond family. The Cymric Celts (Welsh etc.) also used this as a common name. The motto is "Liberty." Variants of this name were the origins of O'Hevegan and Hevecan and of O'Hevie, Hevey etc. The O'Hevecans were of the Ui Fiachrach in Mayo. Éim, -e, *a.*, quick, éimeac, *id.* prompt

Ó fataig, Ó facaig.

O Faughy, O Faghy, O Fahy, O Faye, Faughy, Faghy, Fahey, Fahy, Fay, Foy, from the Gaelic noun-adjective *fohach,* meaning reasonable. A 12th century branch of the Ui Maine, seated at Pobalmuintirfahy (Concourse of Fahy's people) in the barony of Loughrea until the Cromwellian confiscations when many of them migrated to Clare. A branch of the family was also of some consequence in Tipperary.

fát, -a, *pl. id.* and -anna, *m.*, a cause, reason, motive, explanation;

Ó ꝼᴀʟʟᴀṁᴀɪɴ, Ó ꝼᴀʟʟᴀɴᴊᴀꝼꝼ.

O Fallone, O Fallowne, O Fallon, Fallon, Faloon, Falloon, Fallon, from the Gaelic *folloonas,* meaning authority, sway. It is therefore generally translated *descended from the ruler.* The surname was founded before the end of the 10th century. There are several important families such as: O Fallon of Offaly, chiefs of Crioch na Ceadach, now Castlejordan; O Fallon of Connaught, leaders of Clan Uadach once seated at Dysart in the barony of Athlone.

> ꝼoʟʟᴀṁɴᴀꝛ, -ᴀɪꝛ, *m.,* sway, supremacy, authority

Ó ꝼᴀɪʟḃᴇ, Ó ꝼᴀɪʟḃᴇ.

O Falvie, O Falvy, O Failie, O Falvey, Falvey, Fealy, Fealey, from the Gaelic *failve,* (lively). This family was founded in Kerry in the 10th century where its heads were chiefs of Corca Bhuibne now the barony of Corcaguiny. After being dispossessed by the Anglo-Normans the family migrated to Clare. The motto is "Brave and faithful."

> ꝼᴀɪʟḃᴇ, *indec. a.,* lively, pleasant, sprightly
> ꝼᴀɪʟḃᴇᴀċᴛ, -ᴀ, *f.,* brightness, sprightliness; merriment, cheerfulness.

Ó ꝼɪᴏɴɴᴀɪɴ, Ó ꝼɪᴏɴɴᴀɪꝼ.

O Finane, O Fenane, O Fanane, O Finane, Finnan, Fannon, Fanning, Fannin, Finan, from the diminutive form of the Gaelic *fionn,* (fair or blond). This family was founded in Mayo before the 10th century by the chiefs of Coolcarney. MacFibris is of the opinion that the founders came from the Cinel Eoghain.

> ꝼɪᴏɴɴ, *gsf.* ꝼɪɴɴᴇ, *a.,* white, pale, fair (of hue, hair)

Ó ꝼᴀɪꝛᴄᴇᴀʟʟᴀɪᵹ, Ó ꝼᴀɪꝛᴄᴇᴀʟʟᴀɪᵹ.

O Ferrally, O Farrelly, Farrelly, Farley. The root name is from the Gaelic *farceallach,* meaning well-knit or sturdy. The family had its origin in County Cavan in the 9th century. Its leaders were *coarbs* or stewards of the church properties of St. Mogue until the suppression of the monastries.

> ꝼᴀɪꝛᴄᴇᴀʟʟᴀċ, -ᴀɪᵹᴇ, *a.,* well-knit,
> ꝼᴀɪꝛᴄᴇᴀʟʟᴀċ, -ᴀɪᵹ, -ᴀɪᵹᴇ, *m.,* a stump, a lump; *smt.* applied to a stout, burly person;

Ó FIACÁIN, Ó Fiacáig.

Fehane, Feehan, Feghan, Fehan, Feane, O Fighane, O Feehan. The original name is from the diminutive form of the Gaelic *feeach,* (a raven). The name is ancient and has long been widely prevalent. The Latin motto is "Strong and faithful."

> Fiac, *g.* féic, fiaic, *pl.* fiaca, *m.,* a raven; f. oub, *id.* and crow.

Ó FITCEALLAIS, Ó Ficeallaig

O Fihily, O Fihillie, O Fielly, Fihelly, Fehely, Feehely, Feehily, Feely. From the Gaelic *fihalach,* meaning chess-player. The name originated in southwest Cork before the 10th century. Its founders were chiefs of Tuath O Fithcheallach whose clan domain environed Baltimore.

> Fióceallác, -aige, *a.,* relating to chess, chess-playing

Ó FIANNA, Ó FIANNAIDE, Ó Fianna, Ó Fiannaide.

O Fynea, O Finnee, O Finny, Feeney, Finney, Finny. From the Gaelic *feean,* meaning an army (particularly the ancient standing army, see note). The name is therefore translated *soldier.* It originated with a sept of the Ui Fiachrach which, in the 11th century, was seated at Finghid, in Sligo. During the troubled centuries which followed its bearers were dispersed thru Connaught.

> Fiann, *g.* féinne, *d.* féinn, *pl.* fianna, *f.,* the name of the Irish standing army up to and during the time of Fionn Mac Cumaill

Ó FAOLÁIN, Ó Faoláig.

O Feolane, O Folane, O Whalen, O Whealane, O Phelane, O Fylan, Phelan, Whelan, Philan, Fylan. The root of this name is in the diminutive form of the Gaelic *faol,* meaning wild or wolf-like. The surname originated in the 9th century. Its founders are recorded as lords of the Decies (South Munster) before the Anglo-Norman invasion. A branch of the founding family became of consequence in Leinster, holding domain over Magh Lacha down to the 15th century. The invasion of Elizabeth, Cromwell and the Prince of Orange caused the dispersion of this name thruout Munster and Connaught. In Connaught the O Whelans became affiliated with the O Kellys and O Maddens of Galway.

> Faol, *g.* -oil, *pl.* -a and -ta, *m.,* a wolf
> Faol, -oile, *a.,* wild, untamed

O fionnġusa, Ó fronnġusa.

O Finisey, Finnessy, Fennessy. The root name is composed of the adjective *fionn* (fair) and the genitive form of *gus*, (choice). The name is therefore translated *descended from the fair choice* i.e. one well thought of. It appears in The Annals of Munster as early as the 9th century. Later it became somewhat rare. The Latin motto is "God will help us to do right."

fionn- (fionna-), finn- (finne-): *in compds.* fair

ġuſ, *g.* ġuiſ, *pl.* -ſa, *m.*, strong feeling, inclination, desire.

Ó feaRġuis, Ó feaRġusa
Ó feaRġuiſ, Ó feaRġuſa.

O Fearguise, O Farris, O Farrissa, O Fergus, O Ferris, Farris, Ferris, Farrissy. The root of the name is a compound formed from the Gaelic *farr*, (better) and *gus*, (choice), therefore *the better choice*. The name was founded in the 9th century by sept leaders of west Connaught who became hereditary physicians to the O Malley chieftains and erenaghs to the church property of Rossinver, Co. Leitrim. It later appears in the lists of the Jacobite Army.

feaRR, feaRRa, *a., comp.* of maiċ ; better, best

Ó finn, Ó finn.

O Fionn, O Finn, O Finne, Finn, Finne, Fynn. From the Gaelic *fionn*, meaning fair (of complexion or hair). There were three ancient families of this name: O Finn of Galway, 12th century trustees of the church lands of Kilcolgan; O Finn of Sligo, a Breiffney sept of Lough Gill (Calry); O Finn of Monaghan, chiefs of the Feara Rois. The name is still numerous at the points of origin.

fionn, -inn, *m.*, a fair-haired person, a white animal or thing

Ó fionnaġáin, Ó fronnaġáin.

O Finegane, O Fenegane, Finnigan, Finigan, Finnegan, Fenegan, Fanagan. From the diminutive form of the Gaelic *fionn*, (fair). Founded in the 10th century by the leaders of a sept of the Ui Fiachrach in Mayo, this name extended into the other provinces as early as the year 1450 and by the end of the 16th century it was widely prevalent.

CROM abu

Mac ʒEARAILᴄ, ᵯᴀc ʒeᵴᴘᴀᵹͪᴄ.

MacGarilt, MacGerald, FitzGerald, Fitzgerald. This name is simply the Irish form of the Norman-French surname Fils Gerald or Fitzgerald. In either language it of course means son of Gerald. The founder of this Irish family was Maurice Fitzgerald (son of Gerald, Constable of Pembroke and Nest daughter of Rhys ap Tewdwyr, King of south Wales) who came to Ireland with Strongbow. The Fitzgeralds were among the Norman-Irish families who were bitterly accused by later English invaders of being "more Irish than the Irish themselves." The Gaelic motto of their scroll is translated "Crom to victory." (Incidentlly, Crom was a deity of Pagan Celtic mythology.)

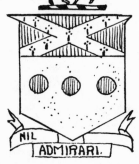

NIL ADMIRARI.

Mac ʒIObÚIn, ᵯᴀc ʒᵼobuᵹͪy.

M'Gibonne, M'Gibowne, MacGibbon, MacGibben, MacKibbon, O Gibbon, O Kibbon, Gibonson, Gibson, FitzGibbon, Fitzgibbon, Gibbons, Gibbins, Gibbings, Gibbon. From the diminutive form of a Gaelic corruption of the Norman-French *Gilbert*. This surname was founded by the head of a 14th century branch of the de Burgos or Burkes of Connaught, whose seat was at Croagh Patrick, County Mayo. Another family of this name was founded in Limerick by Gilbert de Clare in the 14th century. The Latin motto is "Astonished at nothing."

Mac ᵯUIRIS, ᵯᴀc ᵯᴊuᵹͪyᵴ.

MacMorris, MacMorish, McMorrice, MacMaurice, Macmorris, Morrison, Fitzmaurice, Morris. From the Norman-French *Maurice*. This Norman-Irish family was founded by one of the Geraldines who became lord of Lixnaw and played an important part in the history of Kerry. A subdivision of the Prendergasts established a family of this name in Mayo.

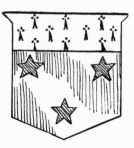

Mac SÍOMÓIn, ᵯᴀc Sᵼoᵹͪoᵹͪy

McShymon, McSimon, Fitzsimon, Fitzsimmons, Simons, Simmons, Symonds, MacKimmons, MacKeemoń, MacKeeman. "Son of Sigemund" (a Teutonic personal name of ancient usage, brought to England and thence to Ireland by the Normans in the form of Simon). The McKimmons and Fitzsimons were substantial families in the City of Dublin by the end of the 15th century.

FORTIS FATISCET.
SUB FORTE

Mac ʒiolla pád́raiʒ, *Mac Ʒiolla Páapaiʒ.*

MacGillephadrich, MacGillapatrick, M'Gillpatrick, MacGilpatrick, MacIllfatrick, MacElfatrick, MacIlfederick, MacElfedrick, Gilpatrick, Kilpatrick, Fitzpatrick. Literally *son of the devotee of (St) Patrick.* The principal family of this name was founded in the 10th century by Gilla Padraigh, son of Donncath, lord of Ossory whose territory embraced parts of the present Counties of Kilkenny and Leix. After the Anglo-Norman invasion much of their territory was ceded to the de Butlers. The Annals record that in 1541 Brian Mac Giolla Padraig was lord of Ossory. Norman-English pressure caused the migration of this family to Clare and Leitrim. The Latin motto is "The brave will yield to the brave."

ʒiollar, -air, *m.*, service; position of ʒiolla

O fláiṫbeaṙṫaiʒ, *O fláiṫḃeaṙṫaiʒ,* O fláiṫiṁ *O fláiṫiṁ*

O Flagherty, O Flaherty, Flagherty, Flaherty, Flaverty. The root name is the compound Gaelic noun-adjective (from *flah* meaning prince and *barthac* meaning performing) *flahvarthac,* generous. The name originated with the chiefs of a sept of Muinntear Murcatha who were seated at the place now called Muntermorroghoe, east of Loch Corrib, County Galway. They were affiliated with the O Kellys of Ui Maine and are recorded in The Annals as early as the 9th century. A variant of this name, anglicized O Flahiff, O Flahie, Flahive and Flahy, from the same root word and with the same clan origin and affiliations became prevalent in Galway, Clare and Tipperary. fláiṫ-ḃeaṙṫač, *a.,* generous, hospitable

O flannaʒáin, *O flannaʒáin.*

O Flannagaine, O Flanagan, Flanagan, Flanigan. The root name is from the diminutive form of the Gaelic word *flann,* meaning ruddy. The most important family of this name was founded by the 9th century chiefs of Uachtartire in Waterford. Their descendants retained control of that district until defeated by the Norman de Powers after the Anglo-Norman invasion. There were several other ancient families of this same name including a branch of the Oirghialla and followers of the O Carrols of Ely, also a sept of Oirghialla, see Flannery. The Latin motto is "I have fought and conquered."

flannne, *g. id., f.,* redness, flush

CERTAVI VICI. ET

COELO POTENTES
SOLO SALO

Ó ꝼꞁᴀᴎᴎᵹᴀꞁʟᴇ,

O Flannylla, O Flannelly, Flannery, Flannally, from the Gaelic *flann*, ruddy and *gaile*, of valor. The name is therefore translated "of conspicuous valor." The Chronicles record the name as being that of a sept of the Ui Fiachrach who were seated at Loch Glinne (Mayo) in the 12th century. Defeated by the invaders they later retreated to Finghid in Sligo.

ꝼꞁᴀᴎᴎ-ꞃᴜᴀᴠ, *a.*, blood-red.

ᵹᴀꞁʟ, valour

Ó ꝼꞁoᴉᴎᴎ,

O Floinge, O Floine, O Flynn, Flynn, Flinn, from the Gaelic *flann*, meaning ruddy or red. The name originated in 8th century Roscommon with the chiefs of Siol Maolruain who held domain in Kilkeevin. A branch of the family became erenaghs (caretakers or trustees) of St. Dachonna's church lands at Eis-O-Floinn, near Boyle, in the 11th century.

ꝼꞁᴀᴎᴎ, -ʟᴀᴉᴎᴎe, *a.*, red, *esp.* in *compds.* a personal name

Ó ᴍᴀoʟᴛᴜꞁꞁe,

O Multilly, O Multully, Tully, from the Gaelic words *maol*, a devotee or servant and *tholl*, the will. It is therefore translated *descended from one devoted to the will* (of God). By confusion of the word *tholl* with *thuill* it has been erroneously translated Flood. The name was founded before the 9th century by the hereditary physicians to the O Connor kings of Connaught. Branches of the founding families later became hereditary physicians to several of the leading clans.

ᴛoꞁʟᴇᴀᴄᴛ, -ᴀ, *f.*, willingness, consent, acquiescence.

Ó ꝼoᵹᴀꞃᴛᴀꞁᵹ, Ó ʜoᵹᴀꞃᴛᴀꞁᵹ,

O Fogarty, O Fogerty, Fogarty, Fogerty, O Hogertie, Hogarty, Hogerty, Hogart, Howard, from the Gaelic *fogar(t)ha*, which means banished or exiled. Of 10th century Tipperary origin, its founders were of the Dalcass. The sept held muster at Eile Ui Fhogarthaigh, now the barony of Elyogarty. The motto: "Rely on heaven alone."

ꝼóᵹᴀꞃᴛᴀ, *p. a.*, announced, proclaimed, warned. outlawed

UT PROSIM.

LUCRUM EST MIHI CHRISTI

O FOSLAÒA

Ó Foġlaòa.

O Folowe, O Foley, Foly, Foley, from the Gaelic *fowla(d)ha,* a plunderer or maurauder. The ancient manuscripts indicate that the surname originated in the present County of Waterford before the 10th century. It later became prevalent in southwestern Eire and attained to some consequence even in the clan Dalcass. The Latin motto is "That I may be of use."

> Foġluġaò, -uiġte, *m.*, act of plundering, spoiling, laying waste ; luċt foġluiġte, plunderers.
> Foġluiġim, -uġaò, *v. tr.*, I ransack, plunder, devastate.

O FUARRÁIN , *Ó Fuaṗṗáiṅ,*
O FUARTÁIN , *Ó Fuaṗtáiṅ.*

O Fuarayne, O Fowrane, O Forhane, O Forhan, O Fourhan, O Forehan, O Forehane O Forane, Fourhane, Forehan, Forhan, Foran, Forde, Ford, from the diminutive of the Gaelic *fuar,* meaning cold. The surname was common to the clans of Thomond and the Decies as early as 980 A.D. It is still widely prevalent in Cork under the form Ford. The motto is translated "To me, Christ is gain."

> Fuaraim, -aò, *v. tr.* and *intr.*, I cool, make cold, refrigerate, give relief to ; I grow cold or cool, become cold or tepid ; I become careless or indevout.

FURLONS , *Fuṗloġg.*

Furlong, Forlong, from the English land measure. An Anglo-Irish family which seized part of Wexford after the English invasion and became of some consequence in Camross, Carrigmanan, Bridestown and Horestown. The motto is "Liberty."

O SAMNA , *Ó Saṁṅa,*
O SAMNAIRE , *Ó Saṁṅaiṗe,*
O SAMNÁIN , *Ó Saṁṅáiṅ.*

O Gowney, O Gaeney, O Gooney, Gaffney, O Gownro, O Goonerie, Gonery, Goonry, O Gownain, O Gownain, O Gownane, Goonane, Goonan, from the Gaelic *gawain* which means a calf. MacFirbis finds that the name originated in a sept of the Clann Muirthuile in Connaught. It is mentioned in the chronicles of the 8th century Norse invasion.

> Saṁain, -ṁna, *pl. id., m.,* a calf

mᴀʒ ᴇᴀᴄᴀʒᴀɪɴ, mᴀʒ ᴇᴀᴄᴀɪꝺ, mᴀʒ ᴇᴀᴄʀᴀɪɴ,
mᴀʒ ᴇᴀᴄᴀʒᴀɪʀ, mᴀʒ ᴇᴀᴄᴀɪꝺ, mᴀʒ ᴇᴀᴄʀᴀɪʒ

mᴀʒ ᴇᴀᴄᴀɪɴ

mᴀʒ ᴇᴀᴄᴀɪʒ

MacGaffigan, Gahagan, Gavaghan, Gavigan, Gavacan, Gaffican, Gaffikin, Gagan, MacGahey, McGahy, MacGaughery, MacGauhy, MacGaggy, MacGaughie, Gahey, Gaffey, McCahey, McGeaghan, MacGahan, Magahan, Megahan, Magann, Geghan, Gaughan, Gahan, Mageachrane, MacGaughran Magaheran, Magahern, MacGahran, McGawran, MacGarran, Gaughran, MacKeough, McKeo, McKehoe, Keogh, all compounds of the Gaelic *eac* or *ach* meaning steed or racing horse, collectively. Founded by an 8th century branch of the O Kellys of Ui Maine whose leaders headed a sept at Mayfinn, the name took the various Gaelic and English forms shown here during its spread thruout the country as its bearers furnished mounted contingents to the national forces opposing the successive waves of invasion. The Latin motto is translated "Always ready to serve my country." ᴇᴀᴄʀᴀᴄ. -ᴀɪʒᴇ, *a.*, abounding in horses. ᴀᴄᴀɪꝺᴇ, *g. ɪᴅ., m.*, a horseman, a jockey ᴇᴀᴄʀᴀɪꝺ, -ᴇ, *pl. id., m.* and *f.* (*coll.*), horses, cavalry

Ó ʒᴀʟʟᴄᴏꝺᴀɪʀ, Ó ʒᴀʟʟᴄᴏꝺᴀɪʀ.

O Galleghure, O Gallagher, Gallagher, Gallaher, Gallogher, Gallangher, Galliher. The root name is formed from the two Gaelic words *gall,* (foreign) and *ca(b)har,* help. This family was founded by a scion of Maolchobha King of Ireland in the 7th century. It furnished military leaders to the forces of the O Donnells and consequently it was prominent in the affairs of northern Ireland for many centuries. It was of special consequence in Tirconnell and played an important part in the turbulent movements of Cinel Connaill from the 13th to the 16th centuries.

ʒᴀʟʟ, *g.* ʒᴀɪʟʟ and ʒᴏɪʟʟ, *pl. id., m.*, a foreigner

ᴄᴀꝺᴀɪʀᴇ, *g. id., pl.* -ʀɪ, *m.*, a helper, assistant, a supporter

Ó ʒɪᴏɴɴᴀɪɴ, Ó ʒɪᴏɴɴᴀɪʒ.
mᴀᴄ ꝼɪᴏɴɴᴀɪɴ, mᴀᴄ ꝼɪᴏɴɴᴀɪʒ.

McKynnan, McKennan, Kennan, Kinnan, from the diminutive form of the Gaelic *fionn* meaning fair. The family originated in a clan of that name in Argyleshire, Scotland. Its founders migrated to Tyrone with the Scotch gallowglasses of the Celtic Alliance.

O Ganon, O Gannon and Gannon, a variant of Mac Fionnain. ꝼɪᴏɴɴᴀꝺ, -ɴᴀɪꝺ, *m.*, a white speck

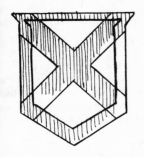

ma5 oireactai5, ma5 Oppeactai5

MacGeraghty, Mageraghty, McGerety, Mac-Gerrity, Geraghty, Geraty, Gerety, Gerity, Gearty, Gerty. The root of the name is in the Gaelic *oireachteas,* meaning an assembly. It is therefore translated "son of the assemblyman." The surname was founded by An-t-Oireac(h)tac O Roduiv of the O Connors of Connaught who founded the sept of Muinntear Roduihv in Roscommon in the 11th century. The sept was later seated in Ui Maine.

> Oireactar, -air, *pl. id.* ana -airi, *m.,* an assembly, a convocation, conference

O 5airdin, O 5appbin.

O Garien, O Garvin, Garvan, Garavin, Garwin, Girwin, Girvin, from the diminutive form of the Gaelic *g(h)arv* meaning rough or rugged. The name originated in a 12th century branch of the southern Ui Neill then seated in Meath. It later became prevalent in Cork and was also found in Sligo.

> 5arb, -airbe, *a.,* rough, rugged, coarse, rude, boisterous

O 5airdeit, O 5appbeit, O 5airdit, O 5appbit.

O Garvie, O Garvey, Garvey, Garvie, from the root word which is compounded from *g(h)arv* meaning rough and *bi(t)h* meaning misfortune or fate. In the 12th century bearers of this name were: (a) Chiefs of Ui Eathach Cobha (now known as Iveagh). (b) Leaders of a sept of the Ui Ceinnsealaigh in Carlow. (c) Members of the Ui Breasail seated in Armagh. The motto is "More wonderful unconquered."

> 5airbe, *g. id., f.,* roughness, coarseness, ruggedness, strength, vigour
> bit, *m.,* fate, misfortune, ill-luck

O 5abain, O 5abairy

O Gavan, Gavan, Gaven, Gavin, from the diminutive form of the Gaelic *gavach,* meaning want or need. The records indicate that this family originated as a branch of the Corca Laoighdhe (west Cork) in the 10th century. Part of this family migrated to Connaught or were exiled there by Cromwell.

> 5abav, -aiv and -bta, *pl. id.* and 5aibte, *m.,* want, need; distress

mᴀ5 ꝼıoɴɴbᴀıʀʀ

mᴀ5 ꝼıoꝈꝈbᴀppꝇ

Maginnoire, McGynnowar, Magennure, Magenor, Geanor, Finbar, Gainer, Gaynor, from the Gaelic compound word *finnevarr* meaning white-top or fair-head. This name originated with a 12th century chief of Muinntear Geara(d)hain in Longford.

ꝼınne, *g. id., f.,* fairness (of hue), whiteness,

bᴀʀʀ-, bᴀʀʀᴀ-, bᴀıʀʀ-, top-, -headed -topped; -haired; -tipped: over-

o 5ᴀoʀᴀ *ó 5ᴀᴘᴀ*

O Garry, O Garey, O Geary, O Geiry, Gwyre, O Gara, Gara, Geary, Guiry, Garry, from the Gaelic *gai(dh)ra,* a mastiff. The family was founded in the 9th century in Connaught where its sphere of influence was near Sliav Luagh whence it was driven to the present barony of Coolhaven (Sligo) after the English invasion of Connaught. The heads of the sept were later lords of Coolhaven. The motto is "Strong and faithful."

5ᴀobᴀʀ, *g.* -ᴀıʀ, *pl. id., dpl.* 5ᴀobᴀıb (5ᴀobᴀʀᴀıb), *m.,* a hound, hunting-dog; beagle, dog, mastiff

o 5ıbeᴀllᴀıɴ, *Ó 5ꝇbeᴀllᴀꝼꝇ.*

O Gibbellayne, O Gibbelaun, Gibulawn, Giblin, Gibsey, Gipsey, Gibson, from the Gaelic *ghioballach,* (tattered). This name was founded in Connaught in the 10th century by a family of Ui Maine who were hereditary custodians of church properties of St Grellawn.

5ıobᴀlᴀċ, -ᴀı5e, *a.,* torn, tattered (of a garment, *etc.*); dressed in tattered clothes (of a person); hairy, woolly

mᴀc 5ıollᴀ bʀı5oe, *mᴀc 5ꝇollᴀ bꝇꝇ5oe*

MacGiollabrida, McGillvrid, McKilbridy, MacElvride, MacGillbride, MacKillbride, Machelbreed, MacBride, Gillbride, Kilbride, from the Gaelic words meaning *son of the servant or devotee of (St) Bridgid.* A common name thruout Eire of the 11th century and afterwards but now more generally found in the north in the form of Macbride. 5ıollᴀ, *g. id., pl.* -ᴀí, *m.,* a lad, a youth, an apprentice, attendant, bʀı5ıo, -5oe, *f.,* a maiden, a fair lady

mac ʒiollᴀ ᴅuiᴅ, *Mac Ʒiolla Duiḃ*.

Mac Giolla Duiv, McGilleduff, McGilleguffe, McGilduff, McKilduff, MacIlduff, McElduff, Gilduff, Kilduff, Duff. The root name is from the Gaelic *mac,* (son) and *giolla dhuv,* (of the black youth). The Chronicles and Annals give evidence that in the 11th century there were three consequential families of this name: (a) MacGiolladuff of Galway who were a sept of the Ui Maine and were chiefs of Caladh in Kilconnell; (b) Mac-Giolladuff of Sligo who were a sept of the Ui Fiachrach; (c) MacGiolladuff of Cavan seated at Tullagairve.

ᴅuiᴅeᴀċt, -ᴀ, *f.,* blackness, darkness

mac ʒiollᴀ ᴅé, *Mac Ʒiolla Dé*.

MacGillegea, McGillegey, McGilgia, Gildea, Kilday, Kildea, Gay, from the Gaelic *macgiolla* (son of the servant) and *dhea,* (of God). The name originated with a monastic family in Donegal in the 11th century. It has always been more or less confined to northwestern Eire. The Latin motto is "Salvation thru the Cross."

ᴅiᴀ, *gen.* ᴅé, *pl.* ᴅéite God

mac ʒiollᴀ ceallᴀiʒ, *Mac Ʒiolla Ceallaiʒ*

McGillakelly, McKillekelly, MacKilkelly, Gilkelly, Killkelly, from the Gaelic words meaning "son of the devotee of St Ceallach" (see Kelly). This family was founded by a son of Guaire, king of Connaught in the 7th century. It was affiliated with the O Clerys and tributary to the Ui Maine. Its sphere of influence was centered at Castle Cloghballymore at Kelleenvarra. The family lost this sphere of influence when Elizabeth's forces defeated the Ui Maine.

mac ʒiollᴀ eᴀspuiʒ, *Mac Ʒiolla Eᴀspuiʒ*.

MacGillaspick, MacGillespie, Gillespie, Gillespey, Gillespy, Galasby, Glasby, Aspig, from the Gaelic *giolla,* a guide, servant or youth and *easbog,* a bishop. The name is recorded in 10th century manuscripts as that of an erenagh family. The motto is "The sure anchor of salvation."

eᴀspoʒ, -puiʒ, *pl. id., m.,* a bishop

Ó ʒıollaʒáın, Ō Ʒʒollaʒáıɣ.

Ó ʒıolláın, Ō Ʒʒolláıɣ.

O Gillegan, O Gilgan, Gilligan, Gillgan, Gillan; and O Gillane, O Gillain, Gillane, Gillan, Gilland, Gillon, Gillen, from *giallain,* a little youth. This family was originally a sept of Cinel Eoghain which became dispersed thruout Galway and Roscommon in the 17th century. The motto is "I am resolved to look upward."

ʒıollanpaıʊ́, -e, *f.,* youths, servants *al.* ʒıollanpaċ.

Mac ʒıolla Máʀτaın, Mac Ʒʒolla Bɣapʒáıɣ.

MacGillamartin, MacGiollavartin, McGilmartin, Gilmartin, Gillmartin, Killmartin, from the Gaelic words meaning "son of the follower of St. Martin." The name is recorded as originating in Ulster where the founders were chiefs of a sept of Cinel Fearaghaigh in the 12th century. By the end of the 16th century it was common in Roscommon and Sligo. ʒıollaṁaıl. -ṁla, *a.,* servant-like.

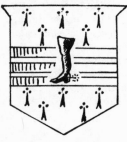

Mac ʒıolla Muıʀe, Mac Ʒʒolla' bɣuɣɣe.

McGillworry, McGilmurry, McGilmore, McIlmurray, MacElmurray, Macmurray, Kilmore, Gilmour, Gilmore, Gilmer, Murray, Murry, from the Gaelic words meaning "son of the servant or devotee of Mary." The name originated in ancient Down where the family was influential in the affairs of Ui Derca Cein and affiliated with the Morna of Lecale. The motto is "Often for my king but always for my country."

Máıʀe, *g. ıd., f.,* Mary

Mac ʒıolla Ruaıʊ́, Mac Ʒʒolla ɣuaıʊ́.

MacGillarowe, McGillaroe, McGillaroy, McKillroe, McKilroy, MacGilroy, MacIlroy, MacElroy, MacAlroy, Gilroy, MacLeroy, Kilroy, Ilroy, Roy. The Gaelic name is formed from the words meaning "son of the red youth." The family was founded in the 11th century by a Fermanagh family seated near Lough Erne. In subsequent generations it spread into Roscommon, Down and Cavan. The motto is "Faithful to the end."

Ruaʊ́-, ʀuaıʊ́-, in *compds.,* red, reddish, brown, red-haired.

O ʒoiᴙmsleaʒaiʒ, Ō Ʒopŋjⁱleaʒaiʒ.

O Gormeley, O Grimley, O Gorumley, O Gormley, Gormilly, Gormley, Grumley, Grimley, from
the Gaelic *gorm,* (blue) and *sleag(h)ach,* (a spear-
man). This name was founded in the 9th century
by the leaders of Cinel Moen, a sept of Cinel
Eoghain which was located in Donegal. In the
13th century they ceded their territory to Cinel
Conaill and assumed control of other lands near
Derry where they retained control until early in
the 17th century when they succumbed to the
English plantation of Ulster. sleaʒ, *g.* -ᴀ, -eiʒe,
f., a spear, javelin
ʒoᴙm-, ʒoiᴙm- blue

O ʒlasáin, Ō Ʒlᴀẛᴀⁱʒ.

O Glassane, O Glesaine, O Gleasan, Glessane,
Glissane, Gleason, Glissawn, Gleesen, from the
diminutive form of the Gaelic word *gloss,* meaning
green. The Annals record the name as existing
in southern Eire as early as the 10th century. The
Gaelic motto is translated "The strong hand uppermost." ʒlᴀᴙ, ʒlᴀiᴙe (ʒluiᴙe), *a.,* green, verdant.

mᴀc ʒoᴙmáin, mᵳac Ʒoᴙⁱⱼᴀẛ.

McGorman, MacGorman, Gor-
man, O Gorman, from the Gaelic *gormawn,* (the
little blue one). It had its origin in Leix in the
9th century when its leaders were lords of Ui
Bairche. In the early years of the Anglo-Norman
invasion the sept was driven from its territory.
Part of it migrated to Monaghan. The greater
part was taken in by the O Briens of Thomond
and was settled at Ibrickan in Clare where it prospered. The heads of this new clan were marshals
of the Thomond armies. After the 15th century
the Munster branch generally took the name O
Gorman while the northern branch retained the
Mac. ʒoᴙm, *g.* ʒuiᴙm, *m.,* blue, the colour
blue

O cúacáin, Ō Cúꞩcᴀᵳ.

O Coughane, O Cowghane, O Quoghane,
Gough. From the diminutive form of the Gaelic
cuach, a cuckoo. The name existed among the
Ui Fiachrach, in Mayo, since the 13th century.
At the beginning of the 16th century it had spread
to Cavan and Roscommon.
cúaċ, -aiċe, -aċa, *f.,* a cuckoo; a term
of endearment.

O ħuᴀɪпɪᴅᴇ, Ó h-Uᴀɪɼᴁᴅᴇ.

Ó ħuᴀɪ̇ᴛпɪ́п, Ó h-Uᴀɪɼᴛпɪ́ᵹ.

O Honie, O Howny, Hooney, Houghney, O Hownyn, O Hunnyn, Huneen, Houneen, Honeen, Oonin, Green, and Greene, from the Gaelic *uaihne*, green. This name had its origin in the Dal Cass and was of consequence in Thomond as early as the 11th century. A branch of the family became followers of O Laoghaire of Corca Laoighdhe and became numerous in Cork. In these connections the name is frequently noted in The Annals of the Four Masters and the works of Keating.

> Uᴀɪпeᴀᴄᴛ, -ᴀ, *f.*, greenness, verdure

O ᵹɼɪoᴃᴛᴀ, Ó Ᵹɼɪ́oᴃᴛᴀ.

O Greefa, O Griffy, O Grighie, Griffey, Griffy, Greehy, Griffith, Griffin, from the Gaelic *Griovha* meaning Griffin-like or having the courageous qualities attributed to that animal. This name was founded by the leaders of Cinel Cualachta (a Dalcassian sept) in the 10th century. Their domain was in the southeast of the present barony of Inchiquin where they built the castle of Ballygriffey. The motto is: "Wish nothing base."

> ᵹɼɪoᴃ-, ᵹɼɪᴃ-, in *compds.*, griffin-like, valorous; ᵹɼɪoᴃ-ᴀɪᴄeᴀᴄ, a long-clawed monster; ᵹɼɪᴃ-ɼeᴀɼ, a daring warrior;

O ᵹɼuᴀᵹáɪп, Ó Ᵹɼuᴀᵹáɪᵹ.

O ᵹɼúᵹáɪп, Ó Ᵹɼúᵹáɪᵹ.

O Growgane, O Grogaine, Groogan, Groggan, Grogan, from the diminutive of the Gaelic *gruagh*, meaning stern or angry. The early bearers of this name were custodians of church estates (erenaghs) in Roscommon. They later scattered thruout Eire. The motto is translated "Illustrious by valor."

> ᵹɼúᵹᴀᴄ, -ᴀɪᵹe, *a.*, stern, fierce, surly, stubborn,
> ᵹɼúᵹ, -úɪᵹ, *m.*, anger, displeasure, fierceness; ᵹ. пᴀ ᵹᴀoɪᴄe, the rage of the wind; ᵹ. ᴍɪc ᴅé, Christ's wrath;

Mᴀc ᵹɪoʟʟᴀ póɪʟ,

Mᴀc Ᵹɪoʟʟᴀ-Póɪʟ.

McGillaphoill, McGillfoile, McKillphoill, MacGilfoyle, Gilfoyle, Guilfoyle, Kilfoyle and Powell. The root name is composed of the Gaelic words meaning *son of the servant of (St) Paul*. The Chronicles indicate that the founders of this name were chiefs of clan Conlegan in Ely Carroll. Their sphere of influence was at Shinrone in Offaly.

mac ʒoτrava, *mac ʒoιpava.*
mac ʒoτraιv, *mac ʒoιpaιv.*

McGorrie, McGorhai, McGorhy, MacGorry, MacGurry, literally *son of Godfrey*. This name was founded by a branch of the Maguires of Fermanagh and became widely prevalent in Ulster.

Ó hEιʒceartaιʒ, *Ó h Éιʒceaptaιʒ.*
Ó hEιʒeartaιʒ. *Ó h Éιʒeaptaιʒ.*

O Heagertie, O Hegertie, O Hagirtie, O Hagerty, Hegarty, Hegerty, Higerty, Hagerty, Hoverty. The root name is from the Gaelic *eigcearthac,* meaning unjust. The founders of this name were members of Cinel Eoghain and descended from Niall of the Nine Hostages. Originally seated in Tyrone the family later moved to Cork where they became numerous. The motto is "I neither bend nor change."

éιʒceapτ, -cιpτ, *m.,* iniquity, a trespass, injustice.

Ó haιlleacáιn, *Ó haιlleacáιn,*
Ó haιlleaʒáιn, *Ó haιlleaʒáιn.*

O Halleghane, O Hallaghan, Hallaghan, Hallihane, Hallahan, Halligan. This name is from the diminutive form of the Gaelic *aille* meaning handsome or beautiful. The Annals indicate that it was common in Ulster in pre-English times and later came into evidence in Cork.

áιllιʒιm, -ιuʒaʋ, *v. tr.,* I beautify, adorn ; I make excellent ; *al.* áιlnιʒιm.
áιlle, *g. id., f.,* beauty (*also* áιlne).
áιlleacτ, -a, *f.,* beauty, loveliness.

Ó hallmuráιn, *Ó hallmuráιn*

O Halowrane, O Halloraine, O Halloran, O Hallaran, O Halleran, O Halleron, Halloran, Holloran. This name is from the Gaelic *allwuran,* a stranger or foreigner (from overseas). Of 9th century origin, this name was that of the clan Feargaile whose seat was near Galway City. Part of this family later became affiliated with the McNamaras of Clare. The name is now common in both counties. The Gaelic motto is translated "Victory to the head of (the clan) Feargail."

allmupac, -aιʒ, *pl. id., m.,* a foreigner.

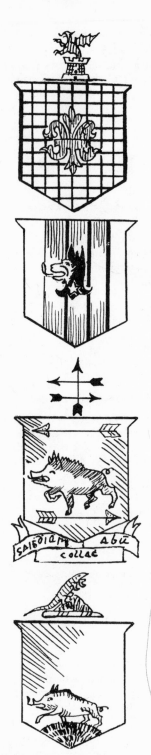

Ó hAilpín,

Ó h-Ailpín.

O Halpin, O Halpenny, O Halfpenny, Halpin, Halpenny, Halfpenny, Halpeny. The root name is the diminutive form of the Gaelic *alp*, meaning a lump. It is therefore translated *descended from the lumpy or stout little person*. The early manuscripts hold that this name originated in County Monaghan. However, it appears to have been well established in Limerick for over five hundred years.　　Alpán, -áin, *pl. id.*, *m.*, a lump; a strong stout man

Ó hAnnagáin, Ó h-Annagáin.

O Hannegan, O Hanigan, Hanagan, Hanigan, Hannigan from the diminutive of *anna(d)h*, (delay). Of County Limerick origin. The Annals indicate that its founders fought against the seizure of Limerick by the Danes and even contested their possession of Scattery Island in the 10th century.　　Anmain, -e, -amna (anamain, fanamain) *f.*, act of remaining, delaying.

Ó hAinle, Ó h-Ainle.
Ó hAinlíge, Ó h-Ainlíge.

O Hanlee, O Hanley, O Henly, Hanley, Hanly, Henly, Handly, from the Gaelic *ainli(g)him*, (I steer), therefore *descended from the steersman*. This name was originated by the leaders of Cinel Dobhtha in Roscommon. This clan was seated in a district coterminus with the present boundaries of Kilglass, Termonbarry Cloontuskert, which in the 11th to the 16th centuries was known as TuahoHanley. The clan was tributary to the O Connor Donn of Connaught until the 17th century. The Gaelic motto is translated "Victory to the heroic soldier."

　　Ainleoir (ainlígteoir), -ora, -rí, *m.*, a steersman, one who directs
　　Ainlígim, -iugad, *v. tr.*, I steer

Ó hAnluain, Ó h-Anluain.

O Hanlowne, O Hanlone, O Handlon, Hanlon, Hanlan, Handlon. The root name is a compound of the Gaelic prefix *an*, (very or great) and *luain*, (light or splendor). The name originated in clan Ui Niallain seated in Armagh. In the 11th and subsequent centuries the O Hanlons played an important roll in the affairs of their province as indicated by frequent reference to them in the Irish Annals.

　　An-, *intens. prefix*, very, when prefixed to adjectives
　　Luan, -áin, *pl. id.*, *m.*, light, radiance, splendour

ó hαnnαιδ, ó hαnnάιn, Ó ḣAᵹᵹαιⱱ, Ó ḣAᵹᵹάιᵹ

Hanna, O Hannaine, O Hanain, Hannon, Hannan, Hanan, Hanon. This name has the same origin and meaning and its bearers have had a parallel history to the O Hanigans. Another O Hanon family whose name became anglicized from the Gaelic *aïngein,* (unborn, caesarian birth) was seated in Galway being of the sept of Siol Anmchada, the kingdom of Ui Maine. The Galway O Hanons carried the O Kelly coat of arms.

Anαιm, I wait, remain, *etc.*

ꞂAnαċⱱ, -α, *f.,* act of remaining, staying, stopping, waiting

ó hαnRαⱱάιn, Ó ḣAᵹᵹⱱάιᵹ.

O Hanrahan, O Hourihan, O Harragan, O Horogan, O Hourigan, O Horigane, O Horgane, Hawrane, O Howrane, Hanrahan, Hourihane, Horrigan, Háran, Horan, Horgan. The root name is the diminutive form of the Gaelic *anra(d)h* meaning a warrior or champion. The name was widely used and in many forms. The most distinguished ancient families of the name were: (a) O Hanrahan of Thomond, a Dalcassian family whose descendants are still numerous in Clare and Limerick. (b) O Hanrahan of west Cork who were erenaghs of Ross. (c) O Hanrahan of Westmeath who were chiefs of Corcaree.

AnꞂαⱱ, -αιⱱ, *pl. ιⱱ.* hero; a champion; a poet next in degree to an ollamh

mαc ᵹιoᴌᴌα ⱱeαcαιꞂ, mαc ᵹιoᴌᴌα ⱱeαcαιꞂ.

McGilledogher, McGilldogher, MacDacker, Harden, Hardy, Harman, Harmon, Harding, from the Gaelic *giolla deachar,* meaning a hard or rugged youth. The name had its origin in the O Donnell clans in the 12th century and flourished in this affiliation for at least 400 years. In the 15th and 16th centuries the name was numerous in Roscommon.

ⱱeαcαιꞂ, -cꞂα, *a.,* difficult, hard, troublesome

ó hαRRαċⱱάιn, Ó ḣAꞂꞂαċⱱάιᵹ.

O Haraghtane, O Harrighton, O Herraghton, Haroughton, Harrington, from the Gaelic *arrachthac,* meaning mighty, tall or powerful. This name was founded by a family of the Ui Maine in the 12th century and flourished in Galway until the 16th century when its bearers were dispersed thruout Munster after the Ui Maine was subdued by the forces of Elizabeth.

AꞂꞂαċⱱαċ, -αιᵹe, *a.,* mighty, tall, powerful

O hARTAZÁIN, Ō ḃ Ꝺꝛꞇꝼꝺy.

O Hartigan, Hartigan, Hartican, from the diminutive form of the Gaelic *Art(h)* (anglicized Arthur), an ancient Irish personal name also the name of a deity in Celtic mythology from the ancient Celtic *Arthos*, (a bear). This family name had its origin in the Dalcass in the 11th century. Its bearers were numerous in the armies of Brian Boru. Dunlang O Hartigan, a leader of Thomond forces, rendered distinguished service in the battle of Clontarf where Brian defeated the Danes in 1014 A.D.

Áꝛꞇ   noble

O hAIRṁeADAIẞ, Ō ḃ Ꝺꝛꝛꞅeꝺꝺꝺꝼꝺꞃꞅ.

O Harvey, Harvey, Hervey, from the Gaelic *airvi(d)each*, (an accountant or reckoner). This surname belonged to a family of the Ui Fiachrach in Connaught. The chronicles connect this family with church affairs.

Áꝛꝛꝛꝛ, vl. áꝛꝛꝛꝛ. v. ꞇꝛ., I count, reckon.

O neocAID, Ō ḃ Ꝼoꞇꝺꝺ,
O neocADA, Ō ḃ Ꝼoꞇꝺꝺ,
O neocAĊ, O ḃ Ꝼoꞇꝺꞇ.

O Hohy, O Hoye, O Huky, Houghy, Hughy, Howie, Howey, Hoey, Huey, Hoye, Hoy, O Hoa, Howe, Howes, Haugh, from variants of the Gaelic *eachach*, which means possessing or abounding in steeds or horses. This family was descended from the 11th century kings of Ulster whose clans continued to be of some consequence in Antrim even after the English invasion. A family bearing this name belonged to Cinel Aonghusa. This family later spread from Leinster into west Munster and Connaught.

eꝺꞇꝺꞇ, -ꝺꞇʒe, a., abounding in horses.

O neiDín, Ō ḃ Ꝼꝛꝺꝼꞃy,
O neiDín, Ō ḃ Ꝼꝛꝺꝼꞃy.

O Hedine, O Headyne, O Heden, O Headen, O Hedian, O Heyden, Hayden, Heyden, Haydin, Haydon, Hadian, from the diminutive form of the Gaelic *eideach*, meaning clothes or armour. An ancient surname common to all Ireland. The Annals indicate that it originated with the first Crusade.

éꝺꝺeꝺꞇ, -ꝺꞇʒ, pl. id., m., clothes, armour

MIRIOR INVICTUS.

SERVA JUGUM.

SAPIENS ASTRIS DOMINA BITUR

FORTIS FIDELIS. ET

Ó haoÚa, Ó ḟAóḋa.

O Hay, O Hewe, O Hugh, O Hea, O Hays, Hays, Hews, Hughes, from the genitive form of the old Gaelic *ao(d)h,* meaning fire. (Also the name of a God in Celtic mythology.) This was a common personal name amongst the Gael. This surname was found in many of the clans from earliest times. The most important houses were (a) the O Hayes of Ballyshannon, a Tirconnell sept called Eis Ruadh; (b) O Hayes of Monaghan, leaders of Fearmaighe; (c) O Hayes of Wexford, of the sept Ui Deaghaidh. In modern times the O Hayes of northern Ireland generally took the name Hughes while those of the south retained the more ancient form. The motto is: "I keep the yoke." Aónaú, *g.* aóanta, *m.,* act of kindling, inflaming

Ó heiliḋe, Ó ḟÉilṗe,
Ó heiliġe-, Ó ḟÉiliġe.

O Healie, O Healy, O Hely, Healy, Hely, from the Gaelic *eileach,* which means scientific, skillful or learned. This name was founded in Sligo in the 10th century. It was borne by a family which then possessed a district bordering on Lough Arrow and had their stronghold at Ballyhely. The motto is "The wise may rule the stars."

ealaóa (*al.* ealaóain), *g.* -an, *pl.* -úna, -óanta, *f.,* an art or science; skill

Ó heaṙáin, Ó ḟeaṗaṗg.

O Harrane, O Haran, O Heron, O Harran, O Haran, O Hern, Haron, Harran, Heran, Herran, Heron, Hearn, Herne, from the Gaelic *earra(d)h,* meaning fear or distrust. It is therefore translated *descended from the little distrustful one.* This surname belonged to an Oriel family whose leaders were lords of Ui Breasail Macha in the 12th century. eaṗaú, *m.,* fear, distrust

Ó heanna, Ó ḟEaṗṗa,
Ó heanaġáin, Ó ḟEaṗaġáiṗ,
Ó heanáin, Ó ḟEaṗáiṗ.

O Heany, O Heney, Heaney, Heany, Heeny, Heney, O Heanagane, O Henegane, Henekan, O Henane, O Hennaine, Honan, Heenan, Hennan, Heanan. The root name and its variants are from the Gaelic *ean,* which means a bird. The surname originated in the 10th century. The most important families were: (a) O Heany of Limerick which belonged to the Eoghanacht; (b) O Heany of Mayo which belonged to the Ui Fiachrach; (c) O Heany of Thomond, a Dalcassian family which furnished several bishops to the sees of Cashel and Killaloe in the 11th, 12th and 13th centuries. The motto is "Strong and faithful." Éan, *g.* éin, *pl.*
éinte, *m.,* a bird,

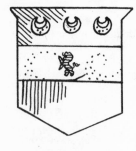

O nifeaRnáin, Ō ḃ ḟreaṗṗáṫ.

O Hifferane, O Hiffernan, O Hifferan, Hifferan, Heffernan, Heffernon, Hefferan, from the diminutive form of the Gaelic *ifrean,* meaning hell. The name is therefore translated *descended from the little hell or little devil.* In the 12th century the O Heffernans were seated at Owneybeg in Limerick where they constituted a sept of Uaithne-Cliach. They were dispossessed by the O Mulryans in the 14th century and were dispersed thruout Munster.

> Iṗreann, -ṗinn, *m.,* hell, the infernal
> Iṗreannaċ, -aiġ, *pl. id., m.,* a demon.

Ó naoláin, Ō ḃṠoláṗṗ.

O Healane, O Hayllane, O Helane, O Hilane, O Hillane, O Hylane, O Heolane, O Hoolan, O Holane, O Hollan, O Holland, Heelan, Helen, Hillane, Hillan, Holan, Heyland, Hyland, Hiland, Holand, from a variant of the Gaelic *faol-con,* meaning a wild dog or wolf, a term anciently indicating cunning and bravery in hunting. It is sometimes anglicized Whelan (which see). This surname was common in middle Ireland in the 14th century. It later spread thruout the country.

> faol-ċú, *g.* -ċon, *d.* -ċoin, *pl.* -ċoin, *f.,* a wolf; a wild dog; a brave warrior

Ó naonġusa, Ō ḃṠaoyṡuṗa.

O Heanesey, O Hennessy, O Hensey, Hennessy, Hensy, Henchy, Hinchy, Hinsy, from the Gaelic *aongus,* meaning first choice. (Also the pagan Celtic god of love.) Starting in the 9th century there developed three important families with this surname: O Hennessy of Thomond, seated in Limerick and Clare and tributary to the O Briens thru the Dalcass; O Hennessy of Offaly constituting a sept of clan Colgan; O Hennessy of Meath bearing allegiance to the Ui Mac Uais.

> Aon, *indef prn.,* one, a single one, only, the only

Ó niarḟlata, Ō ḃ ḟarṗlaṫa.

O Hierlehy, O Herlehy, O Herlihy, Herlihy, Herley, from the compound Gaelic word *iarflath,* meaning an underlord. This was the name of a family of hereditary erenaghs or custodians of church estates. The Annals indicate that the name came into existence in the 12th century.

> Iarḟlaiṫ, *m.,* a feudatory lord; *whence*
> Iarḟlaiṫċeas, a lordship.

Ó heiḋin , Ō ḣ Eḟóiṅ.

O Hein, O Heyne, O Hine, O Hyne, Heine, Hynes, Hyndes, Hines, from the Gaelic ei(d)nean, which means ivy. The bearers of this name were descended from Guaire Eidne who was king of Connaught in the 7th century. The O Hynes were leaders of the Ui Fiachrach Aidhne and held a district coterminous with the present diocese of Kilmacduagh (Galway). The first bearer of this family name, Mulronai O Hines, led a section of the army of Connaught under Tadg O Kelly at the battle of Clontarf in 1014 A.D. and was killed in that engagement.

> Eiḋneán, -áin, m., ivy, a branch of ivy; e. talṁan. ground ivy

Ó huġróin, Ō ḣ Uġróiṅ.

O Hurrone, O Hurrane, O Horan, Horan, from the Gaelic u(g)hrac, meaning bellicose. This family was founded at Clonrush, Galway, in the 12th century. It belonged to the Ui Maine. One of its branches became hereditary coarbs to the church lands of Mayo. A member of this branch was bishop of Elphin in the middle of the 13th century.

> Uġrac, -aiġe, a., bellicose.

Ó huallacáin , Ō ḣ Uallacáiṅ.

O Houlighane, O Holegane, O Holehan, O Houlihan, Houlihan, Hoolihan, Holahan, from the diminutive of the Gaelic ullach, meaning proud. A 13th century Offaly family which later established itself in Cork.

> Uallacán, -áin, pl. id., m., a coxcomb

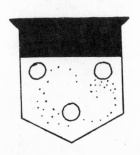

Ó hógáin , Ō ḣ Ōgáiṅ.

O Hogaine, O Hogan, O Hogane, Hogan, from the diminutive form of the Gaelic og, meaning young. This name appears in the records as that of a 13th century Dalcassian family descended from Coscrach, uncle of King Brian Boru. They were seated at Ardcrony, Tipperary. A branch of this family was also located in southwest Cork. The name later became common thruout Munster.

> Ógán, -áin, pl. id., m., a young person of the fourth age, the seven ages being : naoiḋe, leanḃ, macaoṁ, ógán, ḟear, ḟeanóir, aṫlaoc.

Ó hAoḃaġáin, Ó ḡ Áoḃaḡaiɼɼ.

O Hegane, O Higane, O Heagane, Heegan, O Heaken, O Huggin, O Higgins, Hegan, Hagan, Egan, Eagan, Eakin, Higgins, from the diminutive form of the Gaelic *ao(d)h,* meaning fire (also a personal name and the name of a fire god in pagan Ireland). As a personal name it is now translated Hugh. There were two distinct families of this name founded in the 10th century, namely: O Heagan of Monaghan and Armagh and O Heagan of Offaly. See Hayes.

Ó híceaḃa, Ó ḡ íceaḃa,
Ó hícíḋe, Ó ḡ ícíḋe.

O Hickee, O Hickey, Hickey, Hicky, Hickie, from the Gaelic *icea,* meaning a healer. The O Hickeys were members of Dalcass whose name had origin in the 11th century. They were located at Ballyhickey in Clare and were hereditary physicians to the O Briens of Thomond.

> ícíḋe, *g. id., pl.* -óċe, *m.,* a physician
> íceaċ, -cíɣe, *a.,* curing, healing, remedying; -ceaṁail, *id.*

a' cnuic   a' Cġuɼc.

Translated Hill. This is a literal translation. This family name appears in the chronicles of Munster and Connaught as early as the 12th century. The motto is "Let wealth be his who knows how to use it."

> Cnoc, *g.,* cnuic, *pl. id.,* and -a, *m.,* a hill, a height, a mountain

Ó heoḃasa, Ó ḡ Eoḃaɼa,
Ó heoḃusa, Ó ḡ Eoḃuɼa.

O Hoasy, O Hosey, O Hossy, Hosey, from the Gaelic *eo(d)hach,* meaning musical. This was a literary family which had its origin in the Cinel Eoghain in Ulster. Their leaders were once lords of Cinel Tigearnaigh but later became bards to the Maguires of Fermanagh. In the south this name retained approximately its original Gaelic form but in the north it became confused with the Norman Hussey and was sometimes even written Oswell. The motto is "Immovable heart."

> Oḋ, *g.* oiḋe, *d.* oiḋ, *f.,* music, a song
> Oḋaċ, -aiɣe, *a.,* musical

Ó seiteacain, Ó Seiteasoty.

O Sheheghane and translated *Hyde*, from the Gaelic *sheihe*, meaning a skin or hide. This name had its origin in Cork. It appears in church records as early as the 13th century.

> seice, *g. id.*, and -eaó, *d.* -e, -ció, *pl.* -ctí, -eaóa, -eaca, *f.*, a skin or hide,

mac Siúrtáin, mac Siúrtoty.

McShurtayne, McShurdan, McJordaine, Jourdan, Jordan, Jurdan. This name had its origin in the second Crusade. It appears in the Dublin Rolls of the 13th century. Families of the name attained to some consequence in Meath and Limerick in the 15th and 16th centuries. The motto is "Struck down, I arise again."

seóig, Seóig.

Sheoye, Shoye, Joie, Joye, Joy, Joyce, from the Gaelic and old Celtic *sheo*, meaning fun, sport, etc. It may therefore be translated fun-loving or sportive. The founders of this family were Normans of Bretony who came to Ireland via Wales in the 12th century and affiliated with the native Gaels of Galway where they acquired territory and formed a sept in Tuath-Seoghach (Joyce's Country) now the barony of Ross. Hardiman, in his history of Galway, comments on their tallness. The Latin motto is translated "Honor in life or death."

> Seó, *g. id.* and -oig, *m.*, fun, mockery

Ó ceatfaóa, Ó Céatfaóa.

O Keaty, O Keating, Keating, from the Gaelic *ceathfa(d)h,* meaning urbanity. This surname was that of a Dalcassian sept of the time of Brian Boru. They were seated outside Limerick City.

> céatac, -aige, *a.,* reasonable, urbane, =céaofaóac.

ó cᴀoiṁ　ō Caoriǧ.

O Keeve, O Keefe, Keefe, Keeffe, from the Gaelic *caoiv,* meaning beautiful and gentle. This family is descended from Fionhuine, King of Munster in the 10th century. Their original territory was near Fermoy. Driven thence by the Norman Roches they settled at Duhallow when their clan domain was known as Pobul O Keefe until the middle of the 18th century.

> cᴀoṁ-, cᴀoiṁ-, prefixed *a.,* beautiful, gentle; c.-ṛcιᴀċ, a bright escutcheon c.-ċᴀṗᴀ, a dear friend.

ó cᴀollᴀiᴅe,　ō Caollaiᴅe.

O Coely, O Kuelly, O Keally, O Kealy, Keely, Kealy, Quealy, Queely, from the adjective form of the Gaelic *caol,* meaning slender. The Annals indicate that there were several families of this name established as early as the 11th century. The most important were: O Kealy of Kilkenny, chiefs of Ui Bearchon; O Kealy of Tipperary, rulers of Aolmah; O Kealy of Leix, a sept of Crioch O mBuidhe.

> cᴀol, -oιle, *a.,* narrow, slender, thin, graceful, slight; fine, of point, *etc.*

mᴀc eocᴀᴅᴀ　Ṁᴀc Eocᴀᴅᴀ.

McEoghoe, McKeoghoe, MacKeogh, Mac-Keough, MacKeo, MacKough, Keoghoe, Keogh, Keough, from the Gaelic *eocach,* meaning possession of horses. The 14th century families of this name were (a) MacKeogh of Tipperary, chiefs of Owney until dispossessed by the O Mulryans; (b) MacKeogh of Roscommon, a branch of the O Kellys; (c) MacKeogh of Leinster, poets to the O Byrne. The motto is "Stay until you shed your blood."

> eᴀċlᴀċ, -ᴀιǧ, *pl. id.,* *m.,* a horseman, a courier, a cavalryman, *hence* a messen-

ó céileᴀċᴀiṛ　ō Céḟleᴀcιᴀṗṛ.

O Keallaghir, O Kelliher, Kelleher, Kellegher, Kelliher, Keller, from the compound Gaelic word *ceilleacair,* meaning spouse-loving. This family had its origin in the 11th century. Its founder was of the Dalcass, being Donnchuan of clan O Kennedy, brother of Brian Boru. The name finds frequent mention in the chronicles of Thomond.

> céιleᴀċ, -lιǧe, *a.,* mated, sociable, accompanying; *s.m.* and *f.,* a spouse.

TURRIS DEUS FORTIS MIHI

VIR HOSTEM SUPER

O ceallaiʒ, Ó Ceallaiʒ.

O Kelly, Kelly, Kelley, Kellog, Kelloch, from the ancient Gaelic *ceallac,* meaning troublesome or contentious. This family had its origin in the 5th century when Maine Mor descendant of Colla da Crioch led a sept of the Oirgialla from Ulster to Connaught and founded the powerful Ui Maine of which the O Kellys continued to be chiefs until the 18th century. They were hereditary treasurers and leaders of cavalry in the ancient kingdom of Connaught. Tadg More O Kelly, a leader of the Connaught division of the army of Brian Boru, was killed at the battle of Clontarf in 1014. This family lost most of its territory in Galway and Roscommon under Elizabeth. Many of its houses were attainted in 1691 for participation in the Jacobite rebellion. Another family of this name was O Kelly of Breagh affiliated with the southern Ui Neill and seated on the borders of Meath and Dublin. After the Anglo-Norman invasion this family was dispossessed and dispersed. The motto is "God is a tower of strength to me."

> Ceallac -aiʒe, *a.,* troublesome ;

O cinnꝼaolaiʋ, Ó Cinnꝼaolaiʋ

O Kenneally, O Kennelly, O Kineally, Kineally, Kineally, Kennealy, Kennely, from the compound Gaelic word *cinn(f)aolach,* meaning wolfheaded. This family was founded in the 11th century by leaders of Ui Fidgheinte, seated in Ui Connaill Gabhra, now the O Connelloes of Limerick. They were dispersed by the Norman Fitzgeralds but continued to be numerous in Limerick and Kerry.

> Cinn, *a., gs.* of ceann, head-, for the head ; ꝼaol-conʋa, *indec. a.,* wolfish.

O cinnéiʋiʋ, Ó Cinnéiʋiʋ; O cinnéiʋe, Ó Cinnéiʋe.

O Kinedy, O Kennedy, Kennedy, from the compound Gaelic word *cinneadach,* meaning headdressed or helmeted. This family name was founded in the 11th century by Donnchuan, leader of clan Ui Cinneide and brother of Brian Boru of the Dalcass. Seated originally in Killokennedy, Clare, they were later dispossessed by the O Briens and MacNamaras and migrated to Tipperary where in the succeeding centuries they controlled the baronies of upper and lower Ormond. Another family of this name was affiliated with the Ui Maine.

> Cioiʒte, *p. a.,* armed, accoutred, equipped, dressed, garbed.

Ó Cionaoḋa, Ó Cionaoḋa.

O Kenaith, O Kenna, O Kenny, O Kinna, Kenney, Kinney, Kenna, Kenny, from the two Gaelic words *cinn*, (head, source or origin) and *aodh*, fire or the fire god (Celtic mythology). It is therefore translated *descended from the fire god*. A name prevalent in all Eire from earliest times but most numerous in Galway, Limerick, Clare, Roscommon and Tyrone. The motto is "Truth conquers."

Cionaoḋ , fire-sprung,

Ó Ciaragáin, Ó Ciaragáin.

O Kierrigain, O Kerigane, Kerigan, Kerrigan, Kergan, from the Gaelic *ciar*, (black, dark). It is translated *descended from the little dark one*. This name appears first in the 12th century in a branch of the Ui Fiachrach having domain at Ballykerrigan, Mayo. It later spread into Donegal. It is sometimes translated Comber, because of confusion with *cior*, meaning a comb. The motto is "I love my God, my king, and my country."

Ciaraḋ, -ṗḋa, *m.*, act of blackening, darkening, obscuring ; act of waxing.

Mac Tiġearnáin Mac Tiġearnáin.

McKiernane, McKernane, MacKiernan, MacKernan, MacCarnon, MacHarnon, Kiernan, Kernan, Kernon, from the Gaelic diminutive of *thierna*, (a lord). The most important family of this name was founded in County Roscommon in the 12th century by the descendants of Thurlough O Connor, king of Connaught and Ard-ri of Ireland. The Latin motto is translated "Strong and faithful."

Tiġearnaṡ, -aiṡ, *m.*, lordship or dominion, sway,

Ó Cinnsealaiġ Ó Cinnsealaiġ.

O Kynsillaghe, Kinshela, Kinsella, Kinsley, from the Gaelic *cinseallach*, meaning vain, ostentatious. A Wexford family descended from Enna Cinnseallac, son of Dermot McMurrough. The O and the genitive form are not always used.

Cinnrealaċ, -aiġe, *a.*, proud, vain, ostentatious; overbearing

Ó CIARMAIC. *Ó Ciarmaic.*

O Kerwick, O Kervick, O Kervy, O Kerby, Kerwick, Kerby, Kirby, from the compound word *ciarmac,* meaning black (haired) son. Originating in east Limerick in the 10th century this surname was shared by members of Eoghanacht Aine. The Four Masters would indicate that the O Kerwicks of Kilkenny are a branch of this family.

> Ciaṙ, -éiṙe, *a.,* dark
> dark coloured, black ; swarthy

Ó CIARĐUƀÁIN, *Ó Ciardubáin.*

O Kerevan, O Kerrywane, O Kirwan, Kierevan, Kiervan, Kirivan, Kirvan, Kirwan, Kirwin, from the diminutive of the Gaelic compound word *ciarduhv,* which means very black or exceedingly dark complexioned. Originally erenaghs of Louth (12th century) branches of this family became domiciled in Clare and also ranked importantly in Galway City. The French motto is translated "I love my God, my country and my king."

> Đuƀ, dark brown, *al.* very black ;
> cíoṙ-Đuƀ ; c.-ĐONN, dark brown ;

ĐE CNOC, *De Cnoc.*

Cnock and Knox, from the Gaelic *cnoc,* (a hill). This surname was adopted by an early Norman-Irish family in the 12th century. The motto is "In this sign conquer."

> Cnocaċ, -Aiġe, *a.,* hilly, uneven.
> CnocaĐóiṙ, *m.,* a hillman

MAC AN RIĐIRE, *Mac an Ridire.*

McEridery, McIruddery, McRuddery, MacRudderie, MacKnight, Knight, from the Gaelic *ridire,* (a knight). This surname was adopted by branches of the Norman-Irish family of Fitz-Simons of Westmeath.

> RiĐiṙe, *g. id., pl.* -ṙí, *m.,* a knight ; R.
> An Ceampaill, a Templar ;

Ó maolalaid, Ō Maolalaid.

O Mullaly, O Mullally, Mullally, Mullaly, Lally, from the old Celtic *melaglos,* a chief, and the Gaelic *ala(d)h,* meaning speckled. This was the name of leaders of a branch of the Ui Maine in Galway (10th century). They were seated in Loughrea (Maonmhagh) until dispossessed by the Burkes (de Burgos) after the invasion. They then withdrew to Tullanadaly near Tuam. Here they remained until the 17th century when (adhering to the Stuart cause) their leader, James Lally, represented Tuam in the confederation of Kilkenny and sat in King James's parliament in 1689. After the Treaty of Limerick (1691) he was attainted and withdrew to France with his brother Gerald whose descendants, the Counts Lally de Tollendal, distinguished themselves in European affairs.

> Alaḋ, *pl.* Alaṫa, *a.,* coloured variously, speckled, piebald; A.-ḃreac, *id.*

Ó leaṫloḃair, Ō Leaṫlobair.

O Lalour, O Lawler, O Lalor, Lalor, Lawlor, Lawler, from the compound Gaelic word *lea(t)hlo-(b)ar,* (a half-leper). This name originated in the 10th century when its founders were princes of Dalradia. Later the O Lalors were among the "seven septs of Leix" and resided at Dunamase whence they were driven by the English Piggotts during the reign of Elizabeth. In the early 17th century their remaining numbers withdrew to Kerry. The motto is "Brave and faithful."

> Leaṫ, *g.* -A and leiṫ, *d. id.,* leiṫ and leoṫ (*early*), *pl.* -A, leiṫ, *m.,* a half.
> Loḃar, *gsf.* luiḃre, *a.,* leprous, sick; *sm.* a leper.

Ó laiġín, Ō Laiġín.

O Loyne, O Layne, O Leyne, O Lyne, O Lyen, O Lane, O Leane, O Lien, O Lyan, O Leyne, O Lyons, Layne, Leyne, Lyne, Lane, Leane, Lean, Laney, Lyons, from the Gaelic *lai(g)hean,* (a spear). Originally a Galway family seated at Kilconnell in the 13th century. The O Lyons later became hereditary physicians in Clare, Kerry and Kildare. They retained their original sphere of influence until the beginning of the 18th century.

Laiġne leaṫan-ġlara, spears with broad greenish blue heads (such as gave their name to Laiġin, Leinster).

Laiġean, -ġin, *pl. id.,* and -ġne, *m.,* a spear, javelin;

Ó Longáin, Ó Longáiy.

Ó Longane, Ó Langane, Ó Longa, Ó Langan, Longan, Langan, Langin, Long, from the diminutive of the Gaelic *long,* (a ship). It is translated *descended from a little seafarer.* The founders of this name constituted one of the early ecclesiastical families and are recorded in the Annals as erenaghs of Ardpatrick in Limerick and Patrician stewards of Munster. After the English destruction of the Irish monasteries the family dispersed thru Cork and Kerry. Another family of this surname belonged to the Ulster clan of Ui Breasail in Armagh.

Long-, loing-, in *compds.*, ship-, marine.

Ó Lonáin, Ó Longáiy.
Ó Lonagáin, Ó Longagáiy.

Ó Lonane, Ó Lonan, Ó Lonnan, Ó Lannan, Ó Lennane, Lenane, Lanon, Lannon, Lannen, Lannan, Lannin, Lennon, Leonard, Ó Lonagan, Ó Lonegan, Ó Lanegane, Ó Lannegan, Ó Lanigan, Lannigan. Both forms of this name are from the Gaelic *lonn,* meaning blackbird. The surname first appears in the Annals as that of followers of the O Learys seated at Rosscarbery in Cork in the 12th century. A branch of this family seems to have migrated to Wicklow and became erenaghs of Kilranalagh at a very early period. The Latin motto is translated "Faithful to my unhappy country." Lon, *g.* luin, *pl. id., m.,* an ousel, a black-bird.

Ó Lorcáin, Ó Lorcáiy.

Ó Lurkaine, Ó Lorkan, Lorkan, Lorkin, Larkin, Larken, Larkins, from the diminutive of *lorc,* meaning fierce. The three most important families of this surname were as follows: The O Lorkan of Leinster, descended from the Leinster kings was seated at Forth in Wexford until the 12th century; O Lorkan of Armagh, anciently lords of Ui Niallain; O Larkin of Galway of the Ui Maine, O Madden stock. Lorc, *gsf.* luirce, *a.,* fierce, cruel.

Ó Láimín, Ó Láimíy.

Ó Lavine, Ó Lavin, Ó Laven, Lavin, Laven, Lavan, (Hand) from the diminutive of the Gaelic *laiv,* a hand. It is therefore translated *descended from him of the little hand.* This family was anciently among the followers of MacDermott Roe in Roscommon. The name is still prevalent in Mayo. Lám, *g.* láime, *d.* láim, *pl.* láma, *f.,* a hand, *oft.* taken as including the hand to the elbow or even to the shoulder.

O Laoċḋa,

Ō Laoċḋa.

O Leaghy, O Leahy, Leehy, from the Gaelic *loag(d)ha,* heroic. This surname was common in the clans of Thomond even in the 8th century.

> Laoċamail, -ṁla, *a.,* heroic, brave, chivalrous.

O Laoġaire, *Ō Laoġaire.*

O Leary, Leary, from the Gaelic *laogh-aire,* meaning a keeper of calves. This surname was founded in the 10th century by members of Corca Laoighdhe whose domain was in Rosscarbery, west Cork. After the Anglo-Norman invasion they withdrew to Macroom and became tributary to the MacCarthys and domiciled at Carrighnacurra. Their leaders were attainted and executed by the Parliamentarians under Cromwell in 1642. The Gaelic motto is translated "Strong is your king."

> Laoġ, *g.* Laoiġ, *pl. id.,* and Laoġanta, *m.,* a suckling or very young calf.

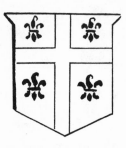

O Laoiḋiġ, *Ō Laoiḋiġ*

O Loye, O Lye, O Leye, O Lie, O Lee, Lee, from the Gaelic *laoi(d)eah,* poetic. A sept of the Ui Briuin Eola, this family was seated in Connaught in the 11th century. The O Lees were hereditary physicians to the O Flahertys and stewards of church domains of Annadown. In the 15th century members of this family wrote a comprehensive medical text in Gaelic and Latin.

> Laoiḋ, -e, *pl.* Laoiċe, -ḋċe, -ḋeanna, *f.,* a lay, poem, or lyric; a song or hymn.

Ō Liatáin, *Ō Liatáin.*

O Lyhane, O Leaghan, O Lehane, Lyhane, Leehane, Leyhane, Lihane, Lyhan, Leehan, Lean, Lyons, from the diminutive of *lia(h),* (grey). This surname originated in the 11th century in Cork from the clan of that name. A Sligo family of the same name belonged to the Ui Fiachrach. The name is now frequently anglicized Lyons.

> Liaċ, *g.* léiċ, *m.,* a grey person, animal or thing.

Ó Leanacáin, Ó Leagacáin.

O Lenaghan, O Leneghan, Leneghan, Lenahan, Lenehan, Lenihan, Lennihan, from the diminutive of the Gaelic *leanach,* meaning sorrowful. This name originated in Roscommon. The chronicles record it as early as the 12th century. The Latin motto is translated "True to my unhappy country."

> Léan, g. -éin, -eoin, d. -éan, -eon
> pl. -nta, m., sorrow, regret, woe.

Ó Loingseacáin, Ó Loingseacáin.
Ó Loingsig, Ó Loingsig

O Lynseghane, Lynchahaun, Lynchahan, Lynchehan, Lynch, O Lynchy, O Lynche, O Lensie, Linchey, Linchy, Lynchy, Lindsy, Lindsay. The root name and its diminutive are from the Gaelic adjective *loingeaseach* meaning, of the fleet or of ships. This race is descended from Loingseach, prince of Dalradia (Ulster) and King of Ireland. The name came into use as a surname in the 10th century. The Annals indicate that a branch of the Antrim family migrated to Clare where their descendants became members of the Dalcass. The name is now common in Donegal, Down, Clare and Limerick.

> Loingeapač, -aiġe, a., abounding in ships.
> Loingpeač, -riġ, pl. id., m., a mariner.

Ó Leannáin, Ó Leagáin.

O Lennane, O Lennan, Linnane, Lannan, Lannon, Lannen, Lennon, Leonard, from the Gaelic *lannawn,* meaning carnal passion, concupiscence. This name originated in Galway in the 12th century with followers of the O Kelly of Ui Maine. A branch of this family became erenaghs of Lisgoole, Fermanagh. The motto is "I come from the best Irish blood."

> Leannán, -áin, pl. id., m., a lover,
> paramour, concubine, favourite, leman.

Ó Lactnáin, Ó Laitgáin.

O Laghnane, O Loghnane, O Loughnane, O Loughton, Laughnan, Loughnane, Loughnan, Loughnane, Loughnan, Lawton, from the Gaelic *lacthna,* meaning greyness. This surname appears in the Annals as that of the chiefs of Clen Nephin, Mayo in the 12th century. Members of this family were bishops in Connaught in the 13th and 14th centuries. Branches of the original family became (a) members of Siol Muireadhaigh; (b) followers of the Ui Maine; (c) erenaghs in Monaghan; (d) coarbs in Meath; (e) chiefs of districts of Longford and Westmeath. The French motto is translated "Loyal to the death."

> Lactna, indec. a., grey, dun, blay.

Ó Lúċaireáin, Ó Luaċra. *Ó Lúċaррeáiη, Ó Luáċpa*

O Logher, O Lucry, Loughry, Loughrey, Lockery, Rush, O Lucherin, O Loghrane, O Loughran, Lougheran. Loughren, Laugheran, Lochrane, Loughrane, Loughran, O Loran, Loran. The root name and the diminutive are from the Gaelic word *luachar,* meaning sedges or rushes (rushlands). The name is therefore translated *of the rushlands.* The chronicles indicate that this originated with hereditary guardians of the church properties of Armagh. Its members were notable in the church affairs of Ulster before the English invasion. The motto is "Virtue always flourishes."

Luaċaiр, -ċpa, *f.,* rushes, sedges.

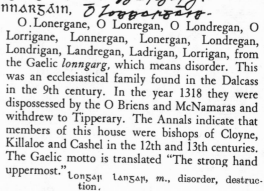

Ó Longargáin, *Ó Longargáiη.*
Ó Lonnargáin, *Ó Lonnargáiη.*

O.Lonergane, O Lonregan, O Londregan, O Lorrigane, Lonnergan, Lonergan, Londregan, Londrigan, Landregan, Ladrigan, Lorrigan, from the Gaelic *lonngarg,* which means disorder. This was an ecclesiastical family found in the Dalcass in the 9th century. In the year 1318 they were dispossessed by the O Briens and McNamaras and withdrew to Tipperary. The Annals indicate that members of this house were bishops of Cloyne, Killaloe and Cashel in the 12th and 13th centuries. The Gaelic motto is translated "The strong hand uppermost." Longaр langaр, *m.,* disorder, destruction.

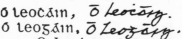

Ó Leoċáin, *Ó Leoċáiη.*
Ó Leogáin, *Ó Leogáiη.*

O Loughane, O Lochan, Loghan, Loughan, Logue, O Lagane, O Lagan, O Logan, Logan, Lagan. The root name and its diminutives are from the Gaelic *leocailleach,* meaning fragile, weak. This name originated with chiefs of the Gailenga Mora and Luighne (now the baronies of Morgallion and Lune) in Meath. In the 12th century the family was dispersed thru Ulster and Connaught. Leoċail, -e, *a.,* delicate, fragile.

Ó Laidgeanáin, *Ó Laidgeanáiη.*

O Laynan, O Loynen, O Leynen, O Lynan, O Leynam, Lynan, Lynam, Lynham, Lyneham, Lineham, Lyman, from the Gaelic *lai(g)hean,* (a spear or lance). The name is translated *descended from the lancer.* This surname had its origin in Carlow (12th century) where its founders were erenaghs of the church property of Ferns. The family later spread thruout Eire in connection with church activities. Laigneaċ, -niġe, *a.,* abounding in spears.

mac amlaoıb, Mac Aṁlaoıḃ.

MacAuliffe, MacAuley, MacCauliffe, Mac-Cauley, MacCawley, MacCowley, Cawley, Cowley, from *mac*, and *a(m)laoiv*, the Gaelic form of the Norse personal name Olaf. The original Irish family of this name was founded in the 11th century by a Norse family which affiliated with the McCarthy of Cork and had its sphere of influence around Castle MacAuliffe near Newmarket. A northern family of this name was a sept of the Maguire and was seated at Clanawly, Fermanagh. The MacAuleys of Antrim are descended from the Scotch family of that name in Dumbartonshire.

mac aoṫa, Mac Aoṫa.

McEa, MacKay, MacKey, MacKee, Mackey, MacCoy, MacHugh, Eason, Hughes, Hueson, Hewson, from the Gaelic *ao(d)h*, meaning fire (also a pagan Irish deity, see Hayes). The principal family of this name originated in Galway and was of the same stock as the O Flahertys, being a leading family in clan Chosraigh. The MacKays of Ulster are descended from the Scottish clan of that name in Strathnaver. The motto is "By the Strong Hand."

O maṫáın, O Maṫáıġ.

O Maddane, O Madden, Madden, from the diminutive of the Gaelic *madha*, meaning mastiff, large dog. This family had its origin in the Ui Maine of Connaught and is descended from Mada(d)an, son of Ga(d)hra More O Kelly chief of the ·Ui Maine. (1014 to 1027) Early in the 12th century the O Maddens became chiefs of Siol n Anmcha(d)ha which had become independent of Ui Maine. They continued in that capacity down to the 18th century. Their sphere of influence was in southeast Galway and that part of Offaly bordering on the Shannon. The motto is "Brave in the cause of justice."

O maṫaṫáın, O Maṫaṫáıġ.

O Madagane, O Madigane, Madigan, Maddigan. A diminutive form of the root name O Madden. The founders of this family came into Clare and Limerick from Galway early in the 16th century. The coat of arms, etc. is that of O Madden. maṫaṫ, *g.* -aıṫ, *pl.* -aṫa, -aıṫe *gpl.* -aṫ, *m.*, a dog.

mac ʒiolla iasacta

Mac ʒiolla Ɉasacta.

McGillesachta, McGillisachia, McGillysaghtie, MacLysaght, Lysaght, Lysat, from the Gaelic *giolla,* (a youth) and *iasachtac,* (strange). It is therefore translated *descended from the strange youth.* It was founded by the descendants of Donaill More O Brien, king of Munster from 1163 to 1194. The name is still common in Clare. The motto is "Salvation thru the cross."

> ɨasácta, *a.*, loaned; strange, foreign; alternative; ɔuine ɨ., a stranger, a foreigner, one not of the household.

maʒ samraɔáin, *Maʒ Samraɔáɉɉ*

maʒ samráin, *Maʒ Sampáɉɉ.*

Magoveran, Magovern, Magawran, Magauran, Magaurn, Magurn, MacGaveran, MacGovran, MacGovern, MacGowran, MacGouran, MacGauran, MacGaurn, Gooravan, Gorevan, Gorevin, from the diminutive form of the Gaelic word *sa(m)hradh,* (summer). The Annals indicate that the name existed in the 11th century in a Breiffney family, chiefs of Tellach Eachach in Cavan. The name is now numerous in all Eire.

> Samraɔ, -aiɔ, *pl. id.*, and -aiɔeacá, *m.*, summer, summer weather.

maʒ aonʒuis. *Maʒ Aonʒuɉʃ.*

maʒ aonʒusa, *Maʒ Aonʒuɉa.*

Maguiness, Maguinness, Magennis, Maginness, MacGuinnessy, MacGuinness, MacGenniss, Meginniss, from the Gaelic word *aonguish,* meaning one choice (also the name of the God of love in Celtic mythology, see Hennessy). This family name had its origin in Down in the 10th century. The MacGuinnessy later attained to leadership of Iveagh. The Irish Annals frequently refer to members of this family.

> aonʒuʃ, -a, -uɉʃ, *m.*, Aonghus, the Irish god of love.

mac ɨinn, *Mac Ɉɉʒʒ.*

Maginn, MacGinn, MacGin, MacGing, Meggin, Ginn, McIyn, MacKinn, MacKing. This is an Ulster family of ancient but undetermined origin. The root of the name is in the Gaelic word *fionn,* meaning fair.

> ɨonnaɨm, -áɔ, *v. tr.* and *intr.*, I whiten.

O meacair, O Meacair.

O Meagher, O Magher, O Maher, Meagher, Magher, Maher, from the Gaelic *meachar,* meaning kindly, or affable. This surname had its origin in Tipperary in the 11th century. The founding family was in possession of Druim Saileach near Roscrea. They were of Ely O Carroll stock. After the Anglo-Norman invasion their sept became tributary to Ormond.

> miocair, -e, *a.,* kind, friendly, loving, affable, mild.

O matgamna, O Matgamna.

O Mahowny, O Mahown, O Mahony, Mahony, Mahon, Maughan, from the genitive form of the Gaelic *ma(t)hgaman,* a bear. This family name originated with Mathgaman, son of Cian who was slain at Clontarf in 1014 while leading the Desmond division of the Irish Army against the Danish forces. The O Mahonys were leaders of Cinel mBeice, now known as Kinelmeaky, in Cork and, later, acquired part of the lands of Corca Lauighdhe. The motto is "We guard ourselves and our faith."

> matgamain, g. -mna, *pl. id.* and -mnai, *m.,* a bear.

O meallain, O Meallain.

O Meallane, O Mellane, O Mallane, O Mellon, Mellan, Mellon, Mallan, Mallen, Mullen, from the Gaelic *meallaire,* a deceiver or one who beguiles. This surname was first used by a 10th century branch of the Cinel Eoghain who were hereditary keepers of the Bell of Saint Patrick and were located at Dungannon, Tyrone. The Gaelic motto is translated "Wisdom without blemish." meallaire, g. id,, *pl.* -ri, *m.,* a deceiver.

O maolmuaid, O Maolmuaid.

O Molwye, O Meloy, O Molloye, O Mulloye, O Molley, Meloy, Molloy, Mulloy, from the Gaelic *maolmuadh,* a great leader. This surname originated in Cinel Fiachach in the 10th century. Its founders were descended from Niall of the Nine Hostages. They belonged to the sept of Fearra Ceall whose territory was coterminous with the present baronies of Fircall, Ballycowan and Ballyboy in Offaly. After the invasion the O Molloys became hereditary bearers of the British standard in Ireland, retaining their domains even to the 18th century. Another family of this name belonged to the sept of Taidg-na-h-oidhee in Roscommon. muad, -aide, *a.,* big, great, noble, good.

ó mAoileóin, ó ṁaoileóṫ.

O Mullone, O Melone, O Malone, Malone, from the compound Gaelic word *maoleoin,* meaning *servant of (St) John.* This surname was founded in the 13th century by a church family of Clonmacnoise whose descendants made peace with the English in 1691 and became owners of extensive lands. eoin, *g. id., m.,* John; e. ḃaiſte, John the Baptist; e. ſoiſcéalaíṫe, John the Evangelist

ó mAolḃomnaiġ, ó ṁaolḃoṁṁaiġ.

O Malowny, O Mollowny, O Mullowny, Malowny, Molowny, Mullowney, Moloney, Molony, Muldowny, Muldowney, Muldooney, Downey, Dawney. This surname is from the Gaelic compound word *maoldhomnaigh,* meaning devoted to Sundays, or to the Church. It belonged to a family of the Dalcass beginning with the 11th century. Its sphere of influence was at Tulla in Clare but, later, its members became numerous in Munster. ḋomnaċ, -naiġ, *pl.* -naiġe, -ṁantaiġe, *m.,* Sunday; the Lord.

ó monġáin, ó ṁonġáiṫ.

O Mongane, Mongan, Mangan, Mangin, Mongon, Mannion, Manning, from the diminutive of the Gaelic *mongac,* meaning hairy. This surname originated in Mayo in the 11th century. In later centuries it was shared by two other distinct families located in Fermanagh and Cork. After the 16th century it spread thruout Leinster and Munster. monġaċ, -aiġe, *a.,* maned, long-maned, foaming (of the sea); *al.* flaming, fiery.

ó maine, ó ṁaiṫe,
ó mainnín, ó ṁainṁṫ.

O Many, Many, Meany, O Mannine, O Mannin, O Manynge, Mannin, Mannion, Manion, Manning, Mangin, Mangan. The root name and its diminutive are from the Gaelic *mainne,* meaning failure to act or procrastination. This surname was founded in the 9th century by members of the Ui Maine (descended from Maine More) who formed a sept of Sodhan in Galway and controlled a territory coextensive with the present Tiaquin. Their sept existed for over six hundred years. The leaders were seated at Menlough Castle. Their lands were mostly confiscated in the Cromwellian wars. The name is still prevalent in Galway and Roscommon. mainniġim, -iuġaḋ, -neaċtain, *v. intr.,* I fail, neglect.

O mARCACÁIN, ō mapcaċáŋ, O mARCAIჳ, ō mapcaჳ.

O Markaghaine, O Marcahan, Markahan, Markan, Markham, Ryder. The root name and its diminutive are from the Gaelic *marcach,* a horseman. The chronicles indicate that the family were members of the Ui Maine in the 12th century and later migrated from Galway to Limerick and Clare. The French motto is translated "Always ready."

> mapcaċ, -aiჳ, *pl. id.* and -aiჳe, *m.,* a horseman, a rider, a knight.

mac ALASTAIR, mac Alaſtaŋŋ.

McAlaster, MacAlister, MacAllister, MacCallister, MacEllister, MacAlester, McCloster, MacClester, MacLester, Callister, Lester, from the Gaelic words meaning *son of Alexander.* This name was founded by a branch of the MacDonalds in Antrim in the 15th century. (See Mac Donald.)

mac hAOl, mac ჳhAol.

McCaele, McKeale, McHeale, McHowell, MacHale, Hale, Hales, Howell, Howels, from the Gaelic *aol,* meaning lime-white or bright. This is the surname of a family who came to Tirawley from Wales in the 12th century.

> aol, *g.* soil, *pl.* solta, *m.,* lime; a very bright colour.

mac CÁbA, mac Cába.

McCaba, MacCabe, Macabe, from the Gaelic *cawba* meaning cloaked or hooded. This surname was founded by Norse adventurers who came from the Hebrides in the 14th century and attached themselves to the O Rourke and O Reilly clans as commanders of gallowglass (heavy infantry). They were seated in Breiffney, consequently they are still numerous in Leitrim and Cavan and in the neighboring counties of Monaghan and Meath.

> cába, *g. id., pl.* -í, *m.,* a cape, a coatcollar, a hood, a cloak or robe.

mac aoda buide, Mac áodá buide.

McEabuoy, MacEvoy, MacAvoy, from the Gaelic *aodh,* meaning fire (the Gaelic Fire-god, also a personal name anglicized Hugh) and *bwee,* meaning yellow. The name is therefore translated *son of him of the yellow fire or of the yellow fire-god.* This name is very ancient but I cannot determine the exact point of origin.

buide, *nl.* -ača, *a.,* yellow, tawny.

mac annaid, Mac Aggaid.
mac anna, Mac Aoga.

McAnna, McCanna, MacCanny, Canny, MacAnn, MacCann, from the Gaelic *anna(d)h,* a storm. The Annals show this surname as existing in Munster since the 14th century. The seat of the family was at Drombanny Castle near Limerick until the early 16th century. The motto is "Virtue grows under difficulties."

anaiteamail, -mla, *a.,* stormy, disturbed,

mac artáin, Mac Arcáig.

McArtane, McArtan, McCartane, MacCarten, MacCarton, MacCartin, Cartan, Carton, from a diminutive of the Gaelic *art(h),* meaning a stone, also a popular personal name and the name of a deity of ancient Celtic mythology: The founders of this surname were members of Cinel Faghertaigh in the 13th century and their descendants lived in the district now known as Kinelarty, County Down, down to the end of the 16th century when they were dispersed and scattered thruout Ireland. The Gaelic motto is "I strike."

mac giolla faoláin,
Mac Giolla Faoláig.

McGillallen, MacClellan, MacLellan, MacClelland, MacLeland, Gilfillan, Gilfilland, Kilfillan, Gillilan, Gilliland, Gellan, Gelland, Cleeland, Clelland, Clellond, Leland. Translated literally *servant of (St) Faolan.* The original Irish family of this name were members of the Ui Fiachrach in Sligo in the 11th century. The present Irish name of McClelland came to Ulster after the 16th century.

faoileann, -linn, *pl. id., m.,* a sea-gull;
fig. a graceful woman.

Mag Rait, *Mag Raṫ.*

Magrath, Magragh, MacGrath, MacGragh. Megrath, Magraw, MacGraw, Megraw, MacGra, McCreach, MacRay, MacRea, MacCraith, MacCray, MacCrea, MacWray, Rea, McCraye, McCragh, from the Gaelic *ra(t)h,* meaning gracious or favored. It is therefore translated *son of the gracious one.* The root name was a popular personal name in ancient times. The records show two families of this surname existing before the 13th century. One was in Munster where the McGraths were hereditary chroniclers to one of the houses O Brien. The other was a family of hereditary church land trustees or coarbs of St Daveog having residence at Termon McGrath in Donegal.

Raṫ-, in *compds.,* gracious, favoured, *etc.*

Mac Muirceartaig, *Mac Muirceartaiġ.*

McUrarthie, MacCurdy, MacKurdy, MacKirdy, McMurihertie, McMirirtie, McMoriertagh, McMortagh, McMiertagh, McMurtough, McMurthoe, McMorte, MacMurtrie, MacMurtery, MacMurtry, MacMurdy, MacMordie, MacMutrie, MacMrearty, MacBrearty, MacBrairty, MacMearty, MacMerty, Murtaugh, Murdough, Murdock, Murdow, Murtha, Murta, Murdy, Murt, from the Gaelic *muirceartach,* a navigator. It is evident from the chronicles that this name was in existence in the 8th century altho it perhaps did not become a permanent family name until the early years of the 11th century. Since then it had been widely prevalent, especially in the maritime counties. The motto is "Virtue scales great heights."

Muir-, mur-, in *compds.,* sea-, marine; Ceartuiġṫeoir, -ora, -oirí, *m.,* a corrector, a regulator.

SCANDIT SUBLIME VIRTUS

Mac Diarmada, *Mac Diarmada.*

MacDermody, MacDermot, MacDermonde, MacDerby, MacDiarmod, MacDermott, MacDarby, Dermody, Darmody, Diarmid, Dermid, Dermond, Darby, from the Gaelic *diarmaid,* which anciently meant a common or humble man, was used to denote a typical Irishman and came to be a popular personal name. This surname was first adopted by the children of Dermott Maolruanai son of Tadg O Connor, king of Connaught in the 11th century. The MacDermotts were the sept Maolruanai of the clan Sil-Murray. Their zone of influence was around Mayburg. Their motto is "Always faithful to my friends."

Diarmaid, -ada, *m.,* a male personal name; a typical Irishman.

AMICIS FIDELIS SEMPER

Mac Daiḃeid, Ṁac Daiḃeid.

MacDaveyed, MacDeyt, MacDavid, MacDavitt, MacDaid, MacDevitt, MacDivitt, Davitt, Devitt, Daid, Dake, from the Gaelic form of the personal name David. This surname originated with the children of David O Doherty who was killed in 1208. The family was originally seated in Ulster. (See O Doherty.)

doṁan, -ain, m.; the earth

Mac Domnaill, Ṁac Domnaill.

MacDonaill, MacDonall, MacDonald, MacDonnell, MacDaniel, Donaldson, Donald, from the compound Gaelic word *dhomnaill,* meaning world power. Irish families of this name are mostly descended from Donald, grandson of Somhairle, a 12th century thane of Argyle, Scotland. This branch of the MacDonald clan came to Ireland in the 14th century. In the following 200 years they were engaged in most of the wars and acquired much territory. Another McDonald family was descended from Murtagh More O Brien, king of Ireland. In common with their cousins of Scotland the Irish McDonalds went down with the fall of the Stuart kings. The motto is "Always ready."

Mac Donncaḋa, Ṁac Donncaḋa.
Mac Donncaid, Ṁac Donncaid.

MacDonoghue, MacDonnoghie, MacDonaghy, MacDonchie, MacDenis, MacDonnagh, MacDonough, MacDonogh, MacDonagh, MacDona, MacDunphy, Donoghue, Donohoe, Donaghy, Donogh, Donagh, Dunphy, Duncan, Dennison, Denison, Dennis, from the Gaelic *dhonnca(t)h,* a compound word meaning brown warrior. There were two distinct families of this surname. (a) McDonough of Sligo who were an offshoot of the McDermotts of Moyburg. The manuscript known as the Book of Ballymote was written in part by members of this house. (b) MacDonnoughs of Cork who were located at Kanturk and controlled the district round Duhallow. These were of the same clan as the MacCarthys. The motto is "Glory is the reward of virtue." Donncaḋ brown warrior

Mac Uileagóid, Ṁac Uileagóid.

MacKillegode, MacKilligott, MacElegott, MacElliott, a Gaelic form of the personal name William. This surname was founded in Kerry by affiliation of the 13th century Norman adventurer with a native sept of the McCarthy. The family was originally seated at BallymacElligott but later transferred to Listowel where their descendants were attainted for rebellion in the early part of th 17th cntury.

mac cártaig, mac cápcaig

MacCarhig, MacCarhie, MacCarha, MacCarthy, MacCartie, MacCarty, MacArthy, from the Gaelic *car(t)hac*, which means friendly. This surname originated with Car(t)hac chief of the Eoghanact and descended from Eoghan Mor son of Oilliol Olum, king of Munster in the 3rd century. The father of Car(t)hac was Saorbrehonac, grandson of Cailleachain of Cashel, king of Munster. Saorbrehonac (i.e. free judging) translated to Justin, is still a popular MacCarthy personal name. The MacCarthys, were princes of Desmond until driven from power by the Normans. Thereafter they divided into three powerful clans, namely the MacCarthy of Muskery, the MacCarthy Reagh and the MacCarthy More. Their zones of influence were first Tipperary and later in Cork and Kerry. The motto is "To the brave and faithful nothing is difficult." Capa, g. capao, d. capaio, npl. capaio, cáipoe, gpl. capao, m. and f., a friend.

mac eacmarcaig, mac eocigspcaig.

MacCafferchie, MacCafferkie, MacCaffarky, MacCagherty, MacCaugherty, MacCafferty, MacCaverty, MacCaharty, MacCaherty, MacCaffry, Cafferky, Cafferty, from the Gaelic compound word *achmorchach*, meaning a rider of horses, a horseman. This name was founded in Donegal by a family of O Doherty. The chronicles indicate that the surname was well established in the 14th century. The Gaelic motto is translated "Army and country."

Mapcaióe, g. id., pl. -óte, m., a horseman. a rider.

mac an goill, mac an Foill.

Macingill, MacAgill, MacEgill, MacGill, Magill, Gill, from a form of the Gaelic *gall*, meaning a foreigner. This surname originated in the 12th century by being applied to the members of the first Norman-Irish generation. The most important family of this name were of Dublin County. The motto is "Without end."

gall(a)-, goill-, -gall, in compds., foreign, exotic.

mac gaoite. mac gaoitín,

MacGeehin, MacGeehan, Mageehan, Mageahan, MacGihen, MacGihan, MacGehan, MacGahan, Magahan, Megahan, Gahan, Magean, MacGienie, MacGeehee, MacGee, Magee, McGeehy, from the Gaelic *gao(t)h*, meaning wind. This surname originated in Donegal in the 15th century.

gaot, -oite, pl. -a and -aí, f., wind, air, blast, a draught of air or wind; whizz.

Mac an AIRCINN, *Mac an Aircinn,*
mac an AIRCINNIg *Mac an Aircinnig.*

MacEnarhin, MacEnerin, MacKinnertin, Mac-
Naryn, MacAnern, MacNern, MacNairn, Mac-
Kinerkin, Minnerk, MacAnerney, MacEnerney,
MacInerney, MacNerhenny, MacNerney, Mac-
Nirney, MacNertney, Connerney, Kenerney, Kin-
erney, Nerhenny, Nerney, Nertney, Nirney. The
root of this name is in the Gaelic *arcinneac,* meaning a steward or guardian, particularly of church
lands. This surname antedates the general adop-
tion of Irish family names since the offices of
guardianship of church estates were hereditary in
Ireland, having been taken over by the christian
descendants of the ancient druid .families. The
most important of these families are (a) Mac-
Inerney of Roscommon, erenaghs of St Patricks
Church at Elphin; (b) MacInerney of Thomond,
sometimes keepers of the O Brien conscience.

Aircinneac, *m.,* a church officer; steward
of church lands; in English, "here-
nach." Hence mac an Aircinnig=Mac
Inerney.

mac páidin, *Mac Páidín,*
mac páidin *Mac Páidín.*

MacPaidin, MacPadine, MacPaden, MacPadian,
MacPadden, MacPaddan, MacPadgen, Pattinson,
Patterson, Pattison, Paddison, Padian, Patten, Pay-
ton, McPhaddin, McFaddine, MacPhadden, Mac-
Faden, MacFaddin, MacFadden, MacFeddan,
Faddin, Vadin, Fagin, Fagan, Patterson, Padden,
from the diminutive of the Gaelic form of Patrick.
The Annals indicate that this surname originated
in Mayo and that it was numerous in Ulster at a
very early period.

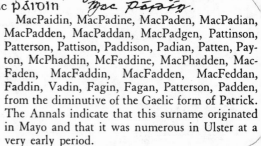

mac inneirge, *Mac Inneirge.*

MacIneirie, MacEnerie, MacKeneyry, Mac-
Keniry, MacEniry, MacNeiry, MacKennery, Mac-
Kenery, MacEnery, MacEnry, Kiniry. This name
is literally translated *son of the riser.* The founders
of this surname were leaders of Corca Muicheat
and resided at Castle MacEniry, County Limerick,
up to the 12th century. They became attainted
after the defeat of the Stuart armies and the
Limerick Treaty of 1691. The Gaelic motto is
translated "The Strong hand uppermost."

éirgim, *vt.* éirge, *fut. etc.* éireoc-; *v.
intr.,* I rise, arise, get up, ascend.

mac ꝼeᴀrᴀꝺᴀıᵹ, Mac ꝼeᴀpᴀꝺᴀꝝᵹ.

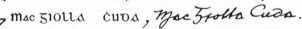

MacKarrye, MacKerry, MacAree, MacKaree, MacCarrie, MacKeary, MacHarry, Maharry, McGarry, MacFarree, MacFarry, MacFerry, MacVarry, MacVerry, from the Gaelic *farra(d)hac,* (manly).' This was originally a popular personal name with the Gael. It was the surname of numerous clansmen of Ulster in the 14th century. The Gaelic motto is translated "A rough man and a good one."

> ꝼeᴀp- (ꝼeᴀpᴀ), ꝼıꝝ-, -ꝼeᴀp (-ᴀp), in *compds.*, a man, man-, male, masculine. manly.

mac ᵹıollᴀ cuꝺᴀ, Mac ᵹꝝollᴀ Cuꝺᴀ.

MacGillacuddy, MacGillecuddy, MacGillycuddy, MacIllicuddy, MacElcuddy, MacElhuddy, from the Gaelic *giolla,* (a servant) and *Mochuda,* an early Irish saint of Lismore. This surname was founded by a branch of the O Sullivan Mor and gave name to the Reeks of Kerry. The leader of the sept was called MacGillycuddy of the Reeks.

mac ᵹıollᴀ eóın, Mac ᵹꝝollᴀ Eóꝝᵹ.

MacEllowen, Magloan, Magloin, Maglone, Malone, MacAloon, MacAloone, MacClune, MacLoone, MacLune, Gilloon, Gloon, from *giolla,* (a servant) and *Eoin,* (John). It is therefore translated *son of the servant or devotee of (St) John.* The local historians locate this name in Tyrone and Donegal where it was numerous in the 14th and 15th centuries.

mᴀᵹ ꝼloınn, Mᴀᵹ ꝼloꝝᵹ.

Maglen, Maglinne, McGlyn, Maglyne, MacGlin, MacGlynn, Glinn, Glynn, from the Gaelic *flann,* meaning ruddy. A Connaught surname recorded also in Ulster in the 14th century. See Flynn.

> ꝼlᴀnn *a.,* red

Mac an ȝoḃa *ṁạc ạɲ ȝoḃa,*
Mac an ȝoḃann, *ṁạc ạɲ ȝoḃạɲɲ.*

MacGowe, Gow, MacAgowne, MacEgowne, MacIgoine, MacIgone, MacGowan, MacGowen, Magowan, Gowen, Gowing, Goan, Smith, Smyth, from the Gaelic *gow,* meaning a blacksmith. Although this name seems to have been generally used in Eire in the 13th century we find no special reference to any sept similarly named with the one exception of Clann Gowann of Clare who were official chroniclers to the O Loghlins of Burren (see O Loughlin).

> ȝaḃa, *g. id.* and -ḃann, *pl.* ȝaiḃne, *m.,*
> a smith, a blacksmith

Mac Riaḃaiȝ, *ṁạc Ríaḃạiȝ,*
Maȝ Riaḃaiȝ, *ṁạȝ Ríaḃạiȝ.*

MacGrevye, MacGreave, Magreevy, Magreavy, MacGreevy, MacGrievy, MacCreve, MacKrevie, MacReavy, MacCreavy, MacCreevy, MacCrevey, from the Gaelic *ria(b)vach,* meaning brindled or speckled. This was the name of a family of the MacDermott clan seated in Roscommon which is mentioned by 14th century historians. The motto is "Faithful to the end."

> Riaḃaċ, -aiḃċe, *pl.* ṁaḃċa, *a.,* brindled,
> striped, tabby, grey, fauve, roan,
> swarthy, grizzled, fallow

Maȝ Uiḋir, *ṁạc Uiḋịrr.*

Maguier, MacGuier, MacGwire, MacGuiver, Maguire, MacGuire, MacGiver, from the Gaelic *a(dh)ar,* meaning pale or duncolored. This surname came into existence in the 19th century in County Fermanagh where its bearers were rulers of an extensive territory and powerful in the councils of Ulster. They became princes of Fermanagh in the middle of the 13th century and remained in power until the reign of James I. They were dispossessed in the confiscation of Ulster. The motto is "Justice and fortitude are invincible."

> Oḋaṙ, *gsf.* uiṫṙe, dun, dun-coloured, pale
> wan, brown, khaki-coloured.

Mac Ioṁair, *ṁạc Ɉoṁạịrr,*
Mac Ioṁair, *ṁạc Ɉoṁạịrr.*

MacEiver, MacKewer, MacIvor, MacIver, MacKiver, MacKiever, MacKever, MacKevor, MacKeever, MacKeevor, MacCure, MacIvers, Ivers, Eivers, Keevers, from the Gaelic form of the old Norse name Ivarr. This surname was founded in the 14th century by a branch of the military clan McDonald of Ulster. The name is still peculiar to northern Ireland.

PRUDENTIA ET HONOR.

mac cionaoda, Ṁac Cionaoda.

MacKinna, MacKenay, MacKena, MacKinney, MacKinny, MacKenny, MacKenna, MacKeany, Kenny, from the Gaelic compound word *cinnaodh,* meaning beloved of Aodh (the fire god). This root name was much in use as a personal name. This surname originated before the 12th century. There were two families of consequence, namely, McKinna of Monaghan, a branch of the Ui Neill, and McKinna of Connaught, followers of the O Connors. The motto is "Wisdom and honor."

cion, *g.* ceana, *m.,* regard, attention, respect, esteem ; affection :

mac eoġain, Ṁac Eoġain
mac eoin-, Ṁac Eoin.

MacOwen, MacEown, MacCone, MacKone, MacKeoan, MacKeown, MacEwan, Keown, Coen, Cowan, Coyne, Owen, Owens, MacEoin, MacKeon, MacKeone, MacKeown, Keon, Keown, from the Gaelic form of the name John. This surname originated in Ulster in the 13th century. Its founders were of the Scottish Bissets who settled in Antrim.

eoġan well-born.

mac ailín, Ṁac Ailín
mac aileáin Ṁac Aileáin.

MacClean, MacElane, MacIlean, MacEllen, Mac-Kilan, MacAlean, MacClean, MacLean, MacKellan, MacKellen, MacKillen, MacAline, MacAlline, MacAllion, MacAllen, MacAllon, MacEllin, Mac-Ellen, Allen, from the diminutive of the Gaelic *ail,* (a rock, cliff or stone). This family is a branch of the Scottish Campbells who came to northern Ireland as gallowglasses for the O Donnells early in the 16th century and settled in Ulster, principally in affiliation with the native clans of Tirconnell.   ail, -eac, *pl.* -tce, -tce, *f.,* a stone, a rock, a boulder

mac loclainn, Ṁac Loclainn.

MacLochlin, MacLoghlin, MacLoughlin, Lough-lin, Loftus. This surname is from the Gaelic *loclainnac,* literally men of the lakes or inlets, a name given to the Norse invaders by the native Irish because of their inclination to remain close to bays, lakes, harbors, etc. This family was a branch of the northern Ui Neill seated at Innishowen up to the 12th century. Part of this group. established an important house in Mayo about the end of the 16th century. The Gaelic motto is translated "The red hand of Eire."

loc, -a, *pl.* id., *m.,* (1) a lake or lough, a pool, a sea-islet.

mac matgamna, Mac Maigamga.

MacMahowna, MacMaghowney, MacKaghone, MacMachan, MacMaghone, MacMaghon, Mac-Maghen, MacMachon, MacMahon, MacMahan, MacMann, Mahony, Mahon, from the Gaelic *ma(t)hgowan,* (a bear). The two great families of this name are: (1) The MacMahon of Clare (members of Dalcass) founded by Mahon, son of Murthagh Mor O Brien, King of Ireland from 1094 to 1119. Their sept was Corca Baiscin, occupying the present baronies of Moyarta and Clonderlaw. The last chief of this clan was killed accidentally at Bearhaven in 1602. Marshall MacMahon, president of France and Duke of Magenta, was a member of this house. (2) The MacMahon of Ulster were part of Oriel and descended from the ancient Oirgialla. The motto of the southern MacMahon is "We guard ourselves and our faith."   matgamain, *g.* and *pl.* -mna. Bear.

mac magnuis, Mac Magguys.
mac magnusa Mac Magguya.

MacManish, MacMoenassa, MacManus, MacManis, Manus, Mannassas, from the Gaelic form of the personal name *Magnus,* a Norse name honoring Charlemagne, which came to Ireland with the Norse invasion. The principal family of this name was founded in Roscommon by Ma(g)nus, son of Thurlough Mor O Connor, Ard-ri of Erie, slain in 1181. A Fermanagh family of MacManus was founded at Senadh Mic Magnusa, (now Belle Isle) Lough Erne, by Ma(g)nus son of Maguire Donn, a chief of Fermanagh who died in 1302. The motto is "Justice and fortitude are invisible."

mac murcada Mac Mupcada.

MacMurroghowe, MacMoroghoe, MacMurphewe, MacMurrough, MacMurrow, Morrowson, Murrough, Morrough, Morrogh, Murrow, Morrow, from the ancient Gaelic personal name *Murca(d)h,* (a sea-warrior). Three great houses bearing this surname existed in Eire before the 12th century. The most important was MacMurrough of Leinster founded by Murca(d)h, grandfather of Dermott McMurrough who was king of Leinster at the time of the first Norman-English invasion. This family long remained powerful in the nation. The MacMurrough of Ulster was of Muinntear Birn and that of Connaught was of Clan Tomaltaigh.

       muineac, -uig, *pl. id., m.,* a sailor or mariner.

Mac Maoláin O Maoláin *Mac Maoláiŋ O Maoláiŋ*

MacMowllane, MacMoylan, MacMullan, MacMullen, MacMullin, MacMullon, MacMillan, MacMillen, Mullin, Mullins, O Mollane, O Melane, O Moylane, O Mullane, O Mullan, Mullane, Mulhane, Melane, Millane, Millan, Mullan, Mullen, Mullon, Mollan, Moylan, from the diminutive of the Gaelic *maol,* bald, or tonsured. The Machouse of this name was founded at Gaile Breagh, Dublin, in the 11th century. The house using the prefix O is a branch which later affiliated with a sept of the O Kane in Derry. The Gaelic motto is translated "Wisdom without blemish."

maol, -aoil, *pl.* -a, state of being bald.

Mac Conmara, *Mac Coŋmaṙa.*

McConmara, MacNamarra, MacNamarrow, MacNamara, from the Gaelic *con-na-mara,* literally *hound of the sea* a name given to a daring seaman. This surname was founded early in the 9th century by a Clare family of the Dalcass deriving its descent from Caisin, son of Cas. They were first located at Ui Caisin but later extended their influence to Upper and Lower Tulla. Their clan name was Clann Cuilinn and their leaders were hereditary marshals of Thomond who had the right to inaugurate the O Brien Kings. The northern branch of the family settled in Down late in the 16th century. Con-, coin-, canine.

Muir, *g.* mara, -rre, the sea.

Mac Conmiḋe
Mac Conmeaḋa, *Mac Coŋmiḋe.*

MacConmea, MacConmay, MacConvea, MacConvey, MacConvay MacConwaie, MacNema, MacConaway, MacNama, Conmey, Convey, MacConamy, MacConomy, MacNamee, Conmee, Mee, Meath, from the Gaelic *cu-mea,* meaning hound of Meath. The original family bearing this name were leaders of Muintear Lao(d)achain in Meath long before the Norman invasion. After they were dispersed their descendants were hereditary poets to the O Neill princes of Tyrone and they are still numerous in Ulster. The motto is "Hope is the anchor of my life." miḋe, *g.* id., *f.,* middle,

with art., an ṁ., Meath.

Mac an ḟailliġiġ, *Mac aŋ ḟailliġiġ.*

MacAnally, MacEnally, MacInally, MacNally, Manally, Canally, Nally, from the Gaelic *failli(g)each,* meaning negligent. This surname originated in Mayo and appears in the Annals in a manner indicating that it was founded by a Welsh-Norman adventurer who affiliated with a native family in the 13th century.

failliġeaċ, -ġiġe, *a.,* negligent, failing.

mac neaċtain, *Mac Neactaiſ*

MacNeaghtane, MacNaghten, MacNaghton, MacNaughton, MacCracken, MacNaught, Mac-Neight, MacKneight, MacKnight, MacNight, Mac-Nite, Mannight, Menaght, Menautt, Minett, Minnitt, from the Gaelic *sneactha,* meaning snow or snow-white. This surname originated in Lochow, Scotland with a family which followed the Mac-Donalds to the Glins of Antrim in the 14th century and became well established in that county and of consequence in the affairs of the nation.

> Sneaċtaiḋe, *indec. a.,* snowy, white.

mac néill, *Mac Néill.*

MacNeill, MacNeile, MacNeal, from the Gaelic *niall,* meaning a champion or otherwise distinguished personage. The native Irish family bearing this surname was part of a sept of Ui Fiachrach with a zone of influence at Carra, Mayo early in the 13th century. The MacNeills of Antrim are descended from the clans of the Lords of the Isles thru the McDonalds of Ulster. The motto is "Thru virtue and sentiment."

> niall, champion

mac an ultaiġ, *Mac an Ultaiġ.*

MacAnulty, MacKnulty, MacNulty, Nulty, from the Gaelic *Ultac,* an Ulsterman. This surname was that of a branch of the O Dunlevys (see note). Originally founded in Donegal, it later took root in Meath and Mayo.

> ultac, -aiġe, *a.,* Ulster, Ultonian;
> *sm.,* an Ulsterman or
> Ultonian, one of the Donlevy family
> (a descendant of the ancient ulaiḋ).

mac seáin, *Mac Seáiġ.*
mac seaġáin, *Mac Seaġáiġ.*

MacSheain, MacSheane, MacShaine, MacShaen, MacShan, MacShane, MacCheyne, Shane, Cheyne, from the genitive of *seagan,* the Gaelic form of John or Jean. This family was founded in Tyrone (MacShane) by the marriage of a Norman knight into a branch of the O Neills. The Annals indicate that the surname was well established in the 14th century. The motto is "Swift and bold."

> Seán, -áin, *pl. id., m.,* John.

mac sítıg, Ɱac Stítıg.

McShihy, McShiehie, McShee, MacSheehy, Sheehy, from the Gaelic si(l)heach, meaning mysterious. This family was founded by Siohach of the MacDonalds of Argyle. The MacSheehys were professional soldiers serving the different Irish and English leaders in Ireland during the 14th, 15th and 16th centuries. The Annals of the Four Masters show them thus engaged even at the end of the 13th century and further indicate that they came to Limerick as constables to Desmond early in the 15th century. They were seated at Lisnacolla near Rathkeale.

Sícheach, -chıge, a., relating to fairies, eerie, mysterious.

mac an beata, Ɱac ag beata, mac an beatan, Ɱac ag beatán.

McEvaghe, McEveighe, McIvagh, McVaghe, McVeha, McVehy, MacAbee, MacIveagh, Mac-Aveigh, MacAvey, MacVeagh, MacVeigh, Mac-Vey, MacVay, MacVea, Vahy, Veigh, from bea(t)ha, (life) therefore translated son of life. While the authorities are vague as to the date of origin of this name, it is fairly evident that it existed in the Oirgialla of Ulster and in the Ui Fiachrach and Ui Maine of Connaught as early as the beginning of the 12th century. Because of some phonetic similarity of the root names the anglicized form has sometimes been confused with MacAvoy. It has been anglicized Vesey in Mayo. The motto is "Thru difficulties."

beata, g. -aú, d. -aıú, pl. -aúa, -aí, f., life, existence.

mac suıbne, Ɱac Suıbġe, Ɱac Suıbġe. mac suıbne,

MacSeveney, MacSwiney, MacSweeney, Mac-Sween, MacSwine, Swiney, Sweeney, McQueyn, McQuine, MacQueen, Maguueen, from the Gaelic suai(m)neac, meaning peaceful or tranquil. Mac-Fibris cites the origin of this surname as originating with Suai(b)ne lord of Argyle whose grandson Murchadh came to Ireland in 1267 and established a family which served as captains of gallowglasses (heavy infantry) to the O Donnell of Tirconnell. In the succeeding centuries the descendants of this family established three great houses namely: MacSweeney of Donegal located at Banagh in the western part of that county; MacSweeney of Fanad, seated at Rathmullin; MacSweeney of Muskerry, commanders of gallowglasses for the MacCarthy of Desmond. The Gaelic motto is translated "Strike to help victory."

Suaımneach, -nıġe, a., quiet, at rest, tranquil, easy, gentle, secure.

TOWOURS PRÈT.

PRODESSE NON NOCERE

PRO FIDE ET PATRIA

mιδeᴄ, mẏṡeaᴄ.

Miache, Meagh, Miagh, Myagh, Meade, from the Gaelic *mi(d)eac,* a resident of Meath. The chronicles record this as the surname of a Norman Irish family residing in Meath in the 13th century and migrating to Cork whence they spread to Kilmallock, Youghal and Kinsale. They are now numerous in Limerick. The French motto is translated "Ever ready."

mιοὑaċ, -aιġe, *a.,* middle.

ó maoᴄáιn, Ō maoᴄaᵹᵹ.

O Meawhan, Meehan, from the Gaelic *mao(t)h,* moist, tearful. This surname shows in the records as being that of a very ancient family seated in Mayo with a zone of influence around Shrule and affiliated with the Ui Maine thru the sept of O Horan.

maoċ, -aoιċe, *a.,* moist, soft, tearful

ó maoιléιᴅιᵹ, Ō maoᴊléιᴅιᵹ

O Mulledy, O Mulleadie, O Malady, Mulleady, Melledy, Meleady, Meledy, Melody, Malady, from the compound Gaelic word *maoleadach,* meaning devoted to clothes. This surname had its origin with a family which, according to the records, resided at Corcumroe, Clare, in the 14th century. The record is silent on the name thereafter until the 16th century when it reappeared in Offaly and branched into Westmeath. The motto is "To do good not evil." éaᴅaċ, -aιᵹ, *pl.* -aιᵹe, *m.,* cloth ; clothes, garments, dress.

ó maoᴅúιn, Ō maoᴅúᵹᵹ.

O Muldoon, Muldoon, Muldon, Meldon, from the Gaelic *maol,* (a chief) and *dhun,* (a fort). It is translated *descended from the commander of garrisons.* This surname originated in a sept of the Feara Luirg at the site of the present Lurg, Fermanagh. The records show the name as dating from the 13th century. Members of this family established branch families in Sligo and Limerick. The motto is "For faith and country."

ᴅún, *g.* ᴅúιn and ᴅúna, *pl.* ᴅúιn, ᴅuιnᴄe, ᴅúnᴄa and ᴅúna, *m.,* a fort, a fortress,

Ó maoilmicil, Ó maoilmicil.
Ó maoilmicil,

O Mulmichell, O Mulvihill, O Mulveill, Mulvihill, Melville, Mitchell, Michail. Literally *descended from the servant of (St) Michael.* This surname was founded by the descendants of Maolviheel, a chief of Siol Murray early in the 9th century. The family's zone of influence was in eastern Roscommon where some of them were chiefs of Corca Sheachlainn prior to the 14th century. Later, branches of the family settled in Kerry, Cork, Limerick and Tipperary. The motto is "For (our) altars and firesides."

míċeál, -ċíl, *m.,* Michael, the Archangel Michael.

mac ʒiolla min, Mac ʒiolla min.
Ó maoilmín, Ó maoilmín.

McGillavyne, McGilvine, MacIlveen, MacElveen, MacKilveen, O Mullivine, Mullveen, Mulveen, Mulvin, Molvin, Melvin. The root word of both forms of this name is *meena,* meaning suave or polite. The name may therefore be translated *suave youth* and *suave leader* respectively. They both originated with the same family, which, as indicated by local records and traditions, has existed in County Down since the 13th century and is of the same stock as the O Mulvaneys.

míne, *g. id., f.,* smoothness, facility, softness, gentleness, fineness, politeness, tameness.

Ó maolaʒáin, Ó maolaʒáin.
Ó maoileaċáin, Ó maoileaċáin.

O Mollegane, O Mullegan, O Mulghan, Mullagan, Mulligan, Mulgan, O Mulleghan, Milligan, O Molaghan, O Mollaghan, Molohan, Mallaghan, Melican, Millican, Milliken, Millikin, O Moylegane, O Milligane, O Mellegan, Milligen, Millican, Melican. The root of all forms of this is the diminutive form of the Gaelic *maol,* bald (not to be confused with *maol,* a chief which comes from the old Celtic *melaglos*). This surname was founded in Tirconnell in the 12th century by members of Tir Mac Carthnainn who were chiefs of a sept located in the eastern part of the present barony of Boylagh. When the sept was dispossessed after the Norman-English invasion its members were incorporated into other independent native clans and in this manner it had spread thruout Eire before the 16th century. The motto is "Strong and faithful."

maolacán, -áin, *pl. id., m.,* anything bald.

Ó maolacáin
Ó maoileaʒáin

ó mocáin, Ó mocáin.

O Mochane, O Moghane, O Muoghane, O Moughane, O Moone, Moghan, Mohan, Moughan, Moohan, Moan, Moen, Mowen, Moon, Maughan, Voghane, Vaughan, from the diminutive form of the Gaelic *moch,* meaning early or timely. This surname was founded by components of Cinel Ianna seated at Kilmacduagh, Galway, in the 12th century and branching into Sligo where they became affiliated with the Ui Fiachrach as erenaghs of Killaraght and custodians of St Attracta's cross. Thereafter they became a distinguished ecclesiastical family devoted to education. Gregory O Voghan was Archbishop of Tuam early in the 14th century. The name is now generally anglicized Vaughan.

moċ, *compar.* moiċe, *a.,* early, timely.

ó manacáin, Ó manacáin.

O Managhane, O Manahan, O Monaghan, Monaghan, Monahan, Manahan, Monk, Monks, from the diminutive of the Gaelic *manach,* (a monk). This surname was established by the descendants of Manachan, 9th century chief of Ui Bruin na Sionna, Roscommon. The family figured importantly in the Barony of Ballintober down to the 17th century. The motto is "The stroked cat is meek." manaċ, -aiġ, *pl., id., m.,* a monk, n tenant of ecclesiastical lands.

ó maonaiġ, Ó maonaiġ

O Moeny, O Mooney, O Moyney, O Money, Meany, Meeny, Mooney, Money, from the Gaelic *maoineach,* (wealthy). The surname was founded in Connaught in the 13th century. The most important houses were: O Meany of Roscommon, chiefs of Clan Murthuile; O Meany of Sligo, members of Ui Fiachrach; O Meany of Galway, belonging to Siol nAnamchadha. During the wars of the 15th century the name spread thruout Eire.

maoineaċ, -niġe, *a.,* rich, wealthy, munificent.

ó móráin, Ó móráin.

O Moraine, O Morane, O Moran, Moran, from the diminutive form of the Gaelic *more,* great. This name originated with a branch of the Ui Fiachrach which controlled sections of Mayo and Sligo in the 12th century. This stronghold was at Ardnaree near Ballina, County Mayo. After bitter resistance to the invaders they were dispersed and scattered thruout Eire in the 15th century. The motto is "They shine in darkness."

mórán, -áin, *pl. id., m.,* much, many, great.

O MÓRDA, Ō mᵹórda.

O Morey, O Mora, O More, O Moore, Morey, More, Moore, from *mor(d)ha,* exalted or great. This family was founded in Leinster, its leaders being chieftains of Leix before the 12th century. Their principal stronghold was Dunamase and they possessed others equally strong thruout their domain. Thus strongly fortified and ably led their clans were able to withstand and repel the attacks of the English for almost 400 years. Under the leadership of Rory O More and Owney O More they inflicted many defeats on the English during the reigns of Mary and Elizabeth. The clan was finally overpowered and in 1609 the remaining O Mores were forced to retire into Kerry whence they later filtered back to their own countryside. The Gaelic motto is translated "Victory to (our) endeavour móρða, *indec. a.,* great, grand, stately, exalted, of high position, proud, noble

O murcáin, Ō mᵹurcáiᵹ.

O Murchan, O Morghane, O Moraghan, Morahan, Morchan, Murchan, Morkan, Morkin, Murkin, Morgan, Morran, Morrin, from the Gaelic *muir,* meaning sea and *caihn,* meaning a rule or ruler. There is evidence that this name had its origin in the 11th century. The principal families were: O Morghane of Connaught, a sept of Ui Maine; O Morghane of Offaly rulers of Magh Aoife. The Connaught family shared in the fall of Ui Maine before the onslaughts of the 15th and 16th century invaders of Connaught. The motto is "I neither wish for nor fear the last day."

muiρ , sea
Cáin, -ána and cánac, *pl.* -eaċa, *f.,* a law, a rule

O muirceartaiᵹ, Ō mᵹuirceartaiᵹ.

O Morierty, Moriarty, Murtagh, Murtaugh, from the Gaelic *muircearthac,* meaning a navigator. This surname originated with a sept of Aos Aisde. Its founders were chiefs of their clan in Kerry before the 13th century and had a zone of influence along the course of the Mang river. The records support the conclusion that the families of this name later founded in Meath and Monaghan were affiliates of this clan. The motto is "Virtue scales great heights."

muiρ·, a sea
Ceaρτuiᵹċe, *p. a.,* corrected, set right, regulated, adjusted, measured.

Ó MAOLRUANAIÓ, *Ó Mjaolruaȝaiȭ*.

Ó Mulruony, Ó Mulrony, Ó Moronie, Mulrooney, Mulrony, Murroney, Morooney, Moroney, from the Gaelic *maol* (ancient Melaglos), a chief and *ruannac,* hairy or bristling. The Annals show four families of this surname originating before the 13th century. They are: Ó Mulrony of Fermanagh who ruled in that territory before the Maguires; Ó Mulroney of Galway, affiliates of Ui Maine, having residence at Cruffan near Ballinasloe; Ó Mulrooney of Clare and Limerick, a sept of the Dalcass (whose surname was early changed to Ó Muruanai by slurring the L sound and was anglicized Moroney); Ó Mulrony of Roscommon who later adopted the name MacDermott. The motto is "Always faithful to my friends."

> Ruainneác, -niȝe, *a.,* hairy, bristly, made of hairs.

Ó MAOLCATAIȜ, *Ó Mjaolcátaiȝ*.

Ó Mulcaha, Ó Mulcahy, Mulcahy, from the Gaelic words meaning *chief of battles.* The chronicles indicate that this surname existed in the clans of Offaly and Thomond as early as the 10th century. It is today common to all Munster and is frequently found in the other provinces. The Gaelic motto is translated "Victory to (our) endeavour"

> Catác, -aiȝe, *a.,* warlike, belonging to battle.

Ó MUIRȜEASA, *Ó Muirȝeasa*.
Ó MUIRȜEASáIN, *Ó Muirȝeasaiȝ*.

Ó Murrissa, Ó Morisa, Ó Morrisey, Morissy, Morrissey, Morrissy, Ó Murghesan, Ó Morrisane, Morrison, Ó Morish, Ó Morris, Ó Morice, Morris. The root name and its variants are from the two Gaelic words *muir,* the sea and *geasaim,* I divine, foretell, or conjure. The translation therefore is *descended from the sea prophet.* The various forms of this surname were adopted by a sept of the Ui Fiachrach which was seated at Sligo Bay in the 11th century and from which branch families were later established in Mayo and Donegal.

> Ȝeaȝaim, -aȭ, *v. tr.,* I conjure divine, foretell   muiȝ, a sea.

Ó MAOLDORAIÓ, *Ó Mjaoldoraiȭ*.

Muldarry, Mulderry, Meelderry, from the Gaelic compound word meaning difficult or troublesome chief. The name originated with a branch of Cinel Conaill in the 9th century. Heads of this house were chieftains in Tirconnell in the three succeeding centuries but the family was almost wiped out in the wars against the invaders. The motto is "In this sign conquer."

> Doraiȭ, -e, *a.,* difficult, difficulty, hardship.

o maoilcatail, Ó ṁaoilċaṫaiḷ.

O Mulcahill, O Molchaill, Mulhall, from the compound Gaelic word meaning servant of St. Cathal. According to authentic records this surname existed in Leix and Offaly since the 11th century. It is now frequently found in other parts of Leinster and in Connaught.

Caṫal, -ail, *m.*, valour; also the name of a man,

o maoilciaráin, Ó ṁaoilċiaráin.

O Mulchieraine, O Mulkerane, Mulkieran, Mulkearn, Mulkern, Mulkerrin, Mulkeeran, Mulheran, Mulherrin, Mulherron, Mulhern, Mulkearns, Mulkerns, from the compound Gaelic word meaning *servant of St Ciaran*. This name was founded by a family of hereditary erenaghs or church estate trustees which became well established in the 9th century. The Annals show that at an early period they were erenaghs of Eaglas Beg, Clonmacnoise, and of Ardcarne in Roscommon. In connection with church affairs, branches of this family became located in Donegal about the end of the 15th century. Like many other great erenagh and ecclesiastical families this house seems to have descended from a family of ancient druids.

o maoileanaiġ, Ó ṁaoileaṅaiġ.

O Mullany, Mullany, Mullaney, from the Gaelic *maoil,* meaning devotee or servant and *seana(d)h,* a synod, senate, (also the personal name of a saint of the early Irish church). This surname originated in Roscommon in the 11th century. The family arbitrated disputes between the clergy and the clans and was seated at Loch Ce. During the next four centuries branches of this family became associated with church activities in Mayo, Sligo and Cork. The motto is "Strong and faithful."

Seanaḋ, -aiḋ, -aiḋe, *m.,* a synod, a senate; Ráiṫ na S., the Rath of Synods (a site at Tara).

o maoilruaiḋ, Ó ṁaoilruaiḋ.

O Melrewe, Mulroe, Mulroy, Mulry, Mulrow, Melroy, Milroy, from the compound Gaelic word *maolrua(d)h,* meaning red chief. This surname had its origin with the family of the Ui Fiachrach. Before the Anglo-Norman invasion the O Mulroe was seated at Ardagh, Tirawley, Co. Mayo. Later the name became common in Galway.

Ruaḋ, -aiḋe, *a.,* red, brownish-red, foxy, red-haired, brown, copper- or bronze-coloured.

Ó maoilmeana, Ó Maoilmeasga.

O Mowlvenna, O Mulvany, Mulvany, Mulvanny, Mulvenna, Mulvenny, Melvenny, from the Gaelic compound word *maoilveanna*, meaning devoted to or concerned with little things or details. This house was founded in Ulster. Its leaders were ollavs to the O Kane. mionac meanac.

mion, *pl.* -a, *m.*, a small thing.

Ó maoilmeaoa, Ó Maoilmeaoa.

O Moylevagh, O Molvay, Mulvagh, Mulvey, from the Gaelic compound word *maoilvegha*, meaning devoted to weighing or measuring. This surname was founded by a 9th century brehon family which belonged to the Dalcass and ruled the sept Cinel mBaoith, being seated at Malbay, Clare. In addition, members of this family were brehons (judges) to the clans of Thomond.

meaoo, *g.* -a and meioe, *d.* meio, mio. *pl.* -a, *f.*, a balance or scales, standard or equivalent; weighing, weight.

Ó murcaoa, Ó Murcaoa.

O Morchowe, O Moroghoe, O Morphy, O Muracha, O Murphy, Murchoe, Murphy, Morphy, from the compound Gaelic word meaning *seawarrior*. In the 12th century there were three distinct families of this name. They are given here in the order of their importance. (1) a branch of Ui Ceinnseallach whose sept was Ui Feilme and was seated at Ballaghkeen in Wexford; (2) a family of Cinel Eoghain who were leaders of the sept Siol Aodha in Tyronne; (3) a house of the Ui Fiachrach which had a zone of influence at Skreen and Templeboy, near Sligo bay, until dispersed in the 13th century. The motto is "Brave and hospitable."

muir- cómrac, a naval engagement cacao, battle.

Ó muireaoaig, Ó Muireaoaig.

O Murrey, O Murry, O Murrihy, Murry, Murray, Murrihy, from the old Gaelic *muirea(d)hai*, meaning a mariner. The ancient manuscripts indicate that this was amongst the first and most numerous of Irish surnames. Its bearers were founders of dynastic and ecclesiastical families as early as the 9th century and surviving as such even to the 15th century. The houses of Mayo, Roscommon and Cork were the most important. The motto is "Faith kept, enriches."

muireac, -rig, *pl. id.*, *m.*, a mariner, maraioe, *g. id.*, *m.*, a seaman.

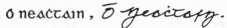

o neactain, O yeactapy.

O Naghtan, O Neaghten, O Naughton, Naughten, Naghton, Naughtan, Naughten, Naughton, Nocton, Natton, Norton, from a variant of the Gaelic adjective *sneathac,* meaning snow-like (a synonym for bright or pure). This surname was founded by a 10th century branch of the Ui Maine which branch, with the O Mulally, at one time formed a united clan, Ui Fiachrach Finn, from Fiachra Fionn, grandson of Maine More who was founder of the Ui Maine and eponymous ancestor to the O Kellys. The O Neaghtans were seated at Maonmagh near Loughrea; County Galway until the 13th century when they resettled at *Fea(d)ha,* Athlone, maintaining a clan at this location until the 16th century. Branches of this family early affiliated with the O Hartigans of the Dalcass. The motto is "You add to the law by serving God."

Sneactac, -taiġe, *a.,* snowy, snow-like, pertaining to snow.

ve nogla, De Nogla.

de Nangle, de Nongle, Nogle, Nangle, Nagle, Neagle. This surname was established in Ireland in the 12th century by the Norman Gilbert de Angulo. The family secured possession of land in Meath and acquired the barony of Navan. Later they shared in the wars of the native Gael against other waves of invasion and were consequently scattered thru Leinster and Munster. The motto is "Not by a voice but by a wish."

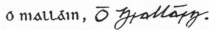

o niallain, O Niallapy.

O Nillane, O Neilane, O Nelane, O Neylane, Nilan, Nelan, Neilan, Nealon, Neylan, Neylon, Nilon, Niland, Neiland, Neyland, Neelan, Neeland, Neelands, from the diminutive of the Gaelic word *niall,* meaning a champion. The chronicles of various districts in western Eire indicate that this surname was established in the Dalcass in the 9th century by a family of ollavs. It later spread to Connaught where, as in Clare, its bearers were at first erenaghs of church property and later became distinguished as an ecclesiastical family. The name is now common in western Clare.

nia, *g.* -ṁ, *d.* -aiṁ, *pl. id.* and -aṁa, *m.,* champion or knight

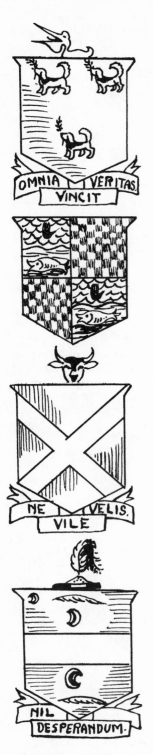

'oe ᴨᴀıs, ᴅᴇ ᵹᴀıᵮ.

de Nasshe, Nash, Naish, Ash, Ashe. This surname came to Ireland in the 13th century (2d) wave of Norman-English invasion. The family settled in Kerry and evolved a substantial Norman-Irish group which, in the later centuries, was of consequence in the affairs of Kerry and Limerick. The motto is "Truth conquers everything."

oe ᴨᴀ́s ᴅᴇ ᵹᴀ́ᵮ.

ó cnᴀ́ıṁsıᵹe, ō Cᵹᴀ́ᵮᴍᵹᴛᵹe.

O Cnawsie, O Knawsie, O Crashie, Kneafsey, Neaphsey, Neecy, Cramsie, Crampsey, Crompton, Crampton, and by translation, Boner, Bonner, from the Gaelic *cnaivsheach,* meaning a midwife. This is one of the rare metronymic surnames found in Ireland. It originated in Donegal and there is evidence that it was well established as early as the 12th century. The root name later spread to Connaught where, particularly in Mayo it took the erroneously translated forms Boner and Bonner. This family originated in Cineal Eoghain.

Cnᴀ́ıṁᵱeᴀ́c, -ᵱıᵹe, -ᵱeᴀ́cᴀ, ƒ., a midwife.

ó cnᴀ́ıṁín, ō Cᵹᴀ́ᵮᵹᵹ

O Knavin, Navin, Nevin, Bowen, Neville, from the diminutive form of the Gaelic *cnaiv,* meaning a bone or bony. This surname was founded by the descendants of Coscrach, son of Lorcan, king of Munster. The family was of the Dalcass and originally seated in Clare but later spread thruout Munster. In west Clare it had generally taken the anglicized form, Neville. The motto is "Never despair." Cnᴀ́ṁ, *g.* -ᴀ́ıṁ, *pl.* -ᴀ́ṁᴀ and cnᴀ́ṁnᴀ, *m.*, a bone; c. ᴀn ᵱᴜ́ᴛᴀ, the fore-arm

ó ᴍᴀᴏ̇, ō ᵹᴦᴀᴏ̇.

O Nee, O Nea, O Ney, O Knee, Nee, Knee, Needham, Neville, from *nea(d)hac,* which means valiant. This surname has existed in Limerick and Kerry since the 9th century. It was established by a church family the head of which was erenagh of Knockpatrick, Limerick. Other branches of the family were concerned with church affairs in Limerick, Kerry and Galway down to the 16th century. The family appears to be of ancient druid origin.

ᴨᴀᴏ̇ᴀ́c, -ᴀıᵹe, *a.*, valiant, brave, strong, stout.

ó nuaðan, Ó Ꝿuaðaꝙ.

O Nowan, O Nowne, Noone, Noonan, from the Gaelic *nua(d)ha,* the name of one of the gods of ancient Irish mythology (adopted by the Celts from the pantheon of their predecessors the De Danann). This surname was that of a Sligo family descended from Caibre, son of Niall of the Nine Hostages. The family controlled the site of the present Calry before the 13th century. The name is now common in Connaught. The Gaelic motto is translated "The red hand of Erin."

> nuaða, -ð, *a.* -aio, *m.,* ancient Celtic God, Noudons; the King of the τuaτa ðé ðanann, and their leader at the battle. of maᵹ τuiṗeað Conᵹa, surnamed ᴀiṗᵹeað-lám
> maᵹ nuaðað, Maynooth

ðe núinnseann, ðe Ꝿunᵹꝿeaðᵹ.

de Nugent, de Nungent, Nugent, from Nogent a common French place name. This Irish surname was established by a Norman family which acquired estates at Winchester, England after the Norman conquest and in the next century were numbered among the Norman-English invaders of Ireland. As allies of the de Lacys the de Nugents acquired property and rank in Westmeath and later became influential in Cork where they formed a clan in the Gaelic manner. The leader of this clan was known as the Uinsheadun (a Gaelic form of the English name Winchester). The seat of the leaders of this clan was at Aghavarten Castle. The motto is "How lovely are thy temples."

ó ꝺriain, Ó ꝺꝛiaꝙ.

O Brian, O Bryan, O Bryen, O Brien, Brien, from the Gaelic *brianach,* meaning variegated or of many qualities. This surname was founded by the grandsons of Brian O Kennedy, historically known as Brian Boru (of the cow tribute) a tenth century leader who became successively, chief of the Dalcass, king of Thomond and King of Ireland and who was killed at the battle of Clontarf (1014) where his national army defeated the Danes and terminated the Danish invasions of Ireland. The O Briens were seated in Clare and in the centuries following the death of Brian they became the most powerful family in Ireland with possessions in Limerick, Tipperary and Waterford. They continued as kings of Thomond until the middle of the 16th century. The name is now one of the most common Irish surnames. The Gaelic motto is translated "The strong hand uppermost."

> ꝺrianać, -aiᵹe, *a.,* variegated.
> ꝺrianna, *pl.,* pieces, bits.

CÓR UNUM VIA UNA.

O ΝUALLÁIN. Ō ŋuallaŋ.

O Nowlane, O Nolane, O Noland, O Nowlan, O Nolan, Nowlan, Nolan, Noland, from the diminutive of *nuall*, meaning Clamour This surname was founded in Carlow in the 10th century by the leaders of Fothart Feadha, the heads of which clan had the hereditary privilege of inaugurating the MacMurrough kings of Leinster. A branch of this sept later settled in west Cork. The motto is "One heart, one way."

> Nuallaim, -aṫ, *v. intr.*, I howl, roar.
> wail; nualluiġim, *id.*
> Nuallán, -áin, *m.*, a cry or howl clamour

O CONAILL. Ō Coŋaṁl.

O Connell, Connell, from the Gaelic *connaill*, which means discreet. The Annals show three important houses of this name existing as early as the 10th century. They are: (1) O Connell of Ui Maine, a branch of the O Kelly, possessing territory in Galway and Clare. (2) O Connell of Kerry, followers of the McCarthy Mor and seated at Cahirciveen (to this house belonged Daniel O Connell, the Liberator, and his uncle Count Daniel O Connell of France, a commander of the Irish section of the French army in the 18th century). The O Connells of Kerry were chieftains of Magh Og Coinchin. (3) O Connell of Derry, a branch of the ancient Oirghialla and rulers of Ui Mac Carthainn. The Gaelic motto is translated "Wisdom and strength."

> Connail, -e, and connla, *a.* discreet.
> friendly.

O ΌEAᴦAIΌ, Ō Ɗeaᵹaiḋ.

O Daa, O Dawe, O Daye, O Deay, O Dea, Dea, Day, Daw, Dee, Godwin, Goodwin, from the Gaelic *dea(g)h,* meaning good, excellent and *a(d)h,* meaning luck or fate. This surname was established in the 9th century by the heads of Ui Fearmaic a sept of Dalcass, seated at Dysart-tola and Tullyodea in the barony of Inchiquin in Clare where, in 1318, their forces so disastrously defeated the Norman-English under Thomas de Clare that Clare was not again invaded for almost 300 years. Descendants of this house are still numerous in Clare. Another family of O Day ruled Sliabh Ardacha (now Slewardagh) in Tipperary before the 13th century.

> Ɗeaᵹ-, ɓeiᵹ-, only in *comp.*, good, excellent, pleasing, virtuous, full; very;
> áṫ, *g.*, áiṫ, áṫa, *m.*, luck, fate, *esp.* good luck, prosperity:

Ó CONCUÜAIR Ó CONCOÜAIR, Ó Cozcuüaip.

O Conchor, O Connour, O Conor, O Connor, Connor, Connors, from the Gaelic con(c)o-(b)arthac, meaning meddlesome. This surname was first assumed by the descendants of Cathoir Mor (king of Ireland in the 2d century) who took the name from Concobair, lord of Offaly who died in 979. The most important groups bearing the name are: (1) O Connor of Connaught, which was descended from the 10th century Connaught king of that name and which furnished two kings to the throne of Ireland. They were divided into three houses, namely: O Connor Donn (brown) O Connor Rua(d)h (Red) and O Connor Sligeach (of Sligo). (2) O Connor of Kerry whose domain was between Tralee and the Shannon until the 13th century when, under pressure of the Anglo-Normans led by Fitzmaurice they retreated to that portion of their ancient territory now known as Iraghticonnor. (3) O Connor of Clare. This family, also of Connaught origin, is descended from Maelseachlainn of Corcomroe who was slain in 1002. (4) O Connor of Derry, rulers of Cranachta until dispossessed by the O Kanes about the beginning of the 12th century. The motto is "I neither fear nor contemn."

Concáüap, -aip, m., Connor,
al. -cuüap.
Concaüaptaċ, -taiże, a., meddlesome

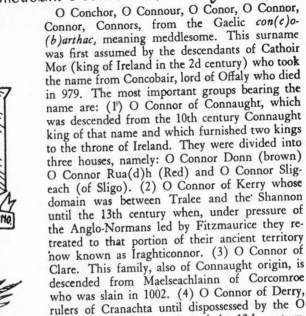

Ó HAIRT, Ó Żaipt.

O Hairt, O Hart, O Harte, Hart, Harte, from arth, (noble) also the name of a god in ancient Celtic mythology. This surname was assumed in the 10th century by a Meath family which resided near Tara. Dispossessed by invaders early in the 13th century, they retreated to Connaught where they became established in Sligo in which county their descendants are still numerous. The motto is "Strong and faithful."

Apt-żloine, f., noble purity

Ó MEAÓRA, Ó Mjeaópa.

O Meara, O Mara, Meara, Mara, from the Gaelic mea(d)air, meaning mirth. The chronicles of Munster record that this surname originated prior to the 13th century in Munster where the family controlled Ros Airguid in Tipperary and where their descendants held possession down to 1692. The family seat was known as Toomyvara. The leaders seem to have occasionally served as brehons to the rulers of Ormond.

meaóap (meaóaip), g. -aipe, -ópa, -ópaċ and meiópe, d. -aip and meióip (al. nom.), f., jollity, mirth, joy; music

ó ꝺoṁnaill, Ó Ꝺoꞃꝝꝝⱥ⫶ll.

O Donill, O Daniell, O Donnell, Donnell, Daniel, from the compound Gaelic word meaning world rock or world strength. (This was also a popular personal name in the ancient clans). The families of this surname are as follows: (1) The O Donnell of Tirconnell who descended from Conall Gulban son of Niall of the Nine Hostages. From the 9th to the 12th century the domain of this clan was confined to the mountains near Lough Swilly but after the Anglo-Norman invasion they became the most powerful Tirconnell clan and under leaders such as Red Hugh they continued to defend their territory against English encroachment for over 400 years and even withstood the repeated drives of Elizabeth's armies. The O Donnells of Tipperary and Limerick are descended from Shane son of Thorlough O Donnell, 15th century ruler of Tirconnell. (2) O Donnell of Clare (seated at Corcabaiscin), founded by Donnell son of Dermott who was killed at the battle of Clontarf in 1014. This family was superseded by the MacMahon in the 14th century. (3) O Donnell of Galway who constituted Clann Flaithea(m)ail which was tributary to the Ui Maine and shared in the subjugation of the O Kellys by the English in the 16th and 17th centuries. (4) O Donnell of Armagh, a sept of the Oirghialla. (5) O Donnell of Carlow, ancient rulers of the clan Ui Drona seated in the territory now known as Idrone. The O Donnells attained distinction as military leaders in Europe during the 15th, 16th and 17th centuries. The motto is "In this sign thou shall conquer."

> Ꝺoṁⱥnꝺⱥ, *indec. a.*, mundane, relating to the world.
> ⱥll, *g.,* ⱥille, *d.* ⱥill, *pl.* -lⱦꞃⱥⱦⱥ, and ⱥilllⱦꞃeⱥⱦⱥ, *f.*, a rock, a cliff.

ó mᴀille, Ó mꝝꝝlle.

O Mailie, O Mallie, O Mally, O Maely, O Malley, O Meally, O Mealy, Malley, Meally, Mealley, Melly, Melia, from the Gaelic *maal,* meaning a noble or a poet (Old Celtic *melaglos,* a chief or a distinguished person). This surname originated with a Mayo family which, in the 11th century, controlled the lands now known as the baronies of Burrishoole and Murresk. Being distinguished for their marine enterprises they were sometimes referred to as Manannans, or sea gods. Another family of this name was seated near the city of Limerick.

> mᴀl, -ᴀil, *pl. id., m.*, a prince or noble, a champion, a poet.

O ᴅonncᴀ1ᴠ, ó ᴅonncᴀ̇ᴅᴀ, O̅ *Oᴏᴈᴈ́ᴀꝗᴅ*, O̅ *Oᴏᴈᴈᴄᴀ̇ᴅᴀ*.

ᴅonn, *a.,* brown

Cᴀ́ᴄᴀᴅ. a battle.

O Donochowe, O Donaghie, O Dunaghy, O Donoghue, O Donohue, Donaghoe, Donoghue, Donohoe, Donaghy, Donagh, Dunphy, Dunfy, Dumphy, from the compound Gaelic word *dhonnca(t)h,* meaning brown battler. The distinct families of this name are as follows: (1) The O Donoghue of Cork and Kerry, who are of the same stock as the O Mahonys, deriving their descent from Eochaidh, son of Cas, son of Cork, who was king of Munster in the 5th century, thru the line of Dubhdabhôireann, king of Munster who (with Cian, ancestor of the O Mahonys) commanded the Desmond division of the Irish Army at Clontarf (1014). The clan names of this O Donoghue were Cinel Laoghaire and Claun Sealbaigh. Their territory originally included part of west Cork but after the 12th century it was restricted to the country surrounding Killarney, now sometimes known as Onaght O Donaghue. The two main sub-divisions of this people were the O Donoghue Mor of Loch Lein residing at Ross Castle and the O Donoghue Glanna (of the glen) residing at Glenflesk. (2) O Donoghue of Connaught, (of O Kelly stock) constituting the sept Ui Cormaic of the clan Ui Maine in Galway. (3) O Donoghue of Ossory who were of the same clan group as the Fitzpatricks, and one of whose leaders founded Jerpoint Abbey in the 12th century. (4) O Donoghue of Meath, rulers of Teallach Modharain the exact location of which is now unknown. (5) O Donoghue of Cavan who were known as Teallach Donncha(d)ha. (6) O Donoghue of Tipperary who with the MacCarthys and O Callaghans derived their descent from Ceallaghain, king of Cashel. Before the 10th century they controlled Magh Feimhin which was coterminous with the present baronies of Iffa and Offa. "Never unprepared." ᴅonncᴀᴅ, *g.* -ᴀᴅᴀ, *m.,* a personal name, Donough, Denis

O hᴀ1ċ1R, O̅ *ɦᴀꝗᴇɦꝗ.*

O Haghie, O Hagher, O Hahir, O Hehir, O Haire, O Hare, Hegher, Hehir, Aher, Hair, Hare, from *acher,* a variant of the Gaelic word meaning angry or irritated. This surname was founded by a 9th century branch of the Ui Fidgheinte of Limerick who settled in Clare at an early date and, before the end of the 11th century, acquired control of Magh Adhair, between Ennis and Tullagh. Later this family moved into Ui Cormaic, west of the Fergus between Ennis and Slieve Callan where their descendants are still numerous.

ᴏ1ᵹᴇᴀꝗ, -ᵹ1ꝗ, *pl.* -ꝗᴀċᴀí . *m.,* irritation,

FORTITER FIDELITER ET

'Oonn　　　*a.*, brown

ʒaɫaċ, -ɑɪʒe, *a.* brave.
　　　　valiant,

VULNERATUS NON VICTUS.

O ɒonnʒaɪle, Ō Ɔoʒʒʒaɪɫe.

O Donnelly, Donnelly, Donneely, from the two Gaelic words *dhonn,* meaning brown and *galach,* meaning valiant. This surname·originated in the 10th century. Its founders were members of Cinel Eoghain and were descended from Donngal who was fourth in descent from Domnall, king of Aileach and brother of Niall Glunghuv, (black knee) ancestor to the O Neills. The family was oríginally located at Drumleen in Donegal but under pressure from Cinell Connaill they re-treated to Ballydonnelly near Dungannon. It was at this location that the O Donnellys fostered the famous Shane O Neill. The family were heredi-tary marshals of the armies of the O Neills. Other families of this surname were: O Donnelly of Sligo, belonging to the Ui Fiachrach and seated at Templeboy. O Donnelly of Cork belonging to Corca Laoighdhe and seated near Dunmanway. The motto·is "Strong and faithful."

O ʒRáɒa, Ā Ʒɾáɒa.

O Grada, O Grady, Grady, Brady, from the Gaelic *gradham,* meaning esteem. This surname was founded in the 12th century by a Dalcassian group located at Killanasoolagh, Clare. About 1318 the family moved to Tomgraney having ob-tained a grant of territory (from the O Briens of Thomond) which included border districts of Clare and Galway formerly held by the O Kellys of Ui Maine. During the reign of Henry VIII part of this family changed their surname to O Brady when their leader, Donogh was knighted by the English king. The family of Donogh was thereafter associated with the English interests. Hugh (O Brady) son of Sir Donogh O Grady was the first Protestant bishop of Meath. The motto is "Wounded but not defeated."

Ʒɾáɒam, -ɑɪm, *m.*, esteem

ANCHORA SALUTIS.

O ɫoċɫaɪnn, Ō ɫoċɫaɪɲɲ.

O Loghlan, O Laghlan, O Loughlan, O Lough-lin, O Loghlen, Loghlin, Loughlan, Loughlen, Loughlin, Laughlin, from the Gaelic *lochlannach,* a foreigner (especially a viking). This surname originated in the 10th century with the descend-ants of Loclann, lord of Corcomroe, Clare. Origi-nally forming one clan with the O Connors of Clare, they ruled over a district coextensive with the diocese of Kilfenora but, afterwards dividing their territory with the O Connors, they retained the west part known as Burren. This they held down to the 16th century. The motto is "The anchor of salvation." ɫoċ·, *f.* and *m.,* ɑ lake

ɫoċɫannaċ, -ɑɪʒ, *pl. id., m.,* a foreigner

Ó heaᵹra, Ó ɧEaᵹᵱa.

O Hara, O Harra, Hara, from a variant of the Gaelic *oi(g)earthac,* meaning bitter or sharp. This surname was founded in Sligo by the children of Eagra, lord of Luighne who died in the year 926. The family was then seated at Leyney where it subdivided into two septs namely the "O Hara Bwee" or yellow O Hara and the "O Hara Riabac" or brindled O Hara. This subdivision occurred in the 14th century. The family was dispersed by the Cromwellian Act of attainder in 1652 which outlawed all of them excepting one house which threw in its lot with Cromwell. A branch of the O Hara settled in Antrim where they attained local importance.

Oiᵹeaᵱċa, *a.*, sharp, bitter, irascible

Ó ouɓuioir, Ō Ɗuɓuᵱóᵱᵱ.

O Duvire, O Duire, O Dwyer, Dwyer, Dwire, from the Gaelic word compounded from *dhuv,* meaning black and *o(d)ar,* meaning yellowish. The name is therefore translated *descended from him of dark tawny color.* The records indicate that this surname originated with a 10th century Leinster family which settled at Coill na Manach (Wood of the Monk) now Kilmanagh, Tipperary. The names of two leaders of this sept, namely Phillip and Owen O Dwyer, were specifically mentioned in the Cromwellian Act of 1652 as being excluded from pardon and thereafter the heads of the family entered the services of Austria, France and Russia, in which countries they attained distinction. The "To hell or to Connaught" policy of the Cromwellian Act above mentioned forced many other members of the O Dwyer clan to move from Tipperary and they apparently settled in Donegal from which they later spread thru western Eire.

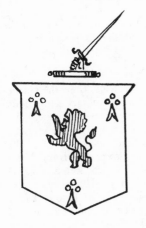

Oóaᵱóa, *indec. a.,* yellowish, light brown.

Ó manannáin, Ō Maᵹaᵹᵹóᵱᵹ.
Ó muᵱnáin, Ō Ṁuᵱᵹóᵱᵹ.

O Manynane, O Mananan, Marrinan, Murnane, Murnain, Murnan, Mornan, Warren, from *Manannan,* a magician of the Isle of Man, son of Lear who was one of the principal sea-gods of pagan Irish mythology. Both the root form of this surname and its variant originated in western Ireland before the 9th century. The Annals indicate that they obtained in several maritime clans of Munster and Connaught. They are especially noted in connection with resistance to Viking invasions of the west coast.

muiᵱ, sea

manannán, *m.,* a magician of the Cuat Oé Oanann, described as a merchant of the Isle of Man, and son of the sea-god; m. mac Liᵱ in full.

MULLACH-A-BU.

Ó Riaʒáin *Ó Riazáry.*

O Riegaine, O Regane, O Regan, Regan, from a diminutive form of the Gaelic *rio(d)gagh,* which means impulsive. The Annals record that this surname was established in Meath by a 9th century branch of the Ui Neill. The O Regans of Meath constituted one of the four tribes of Tara and were powerful in Leinster prior to the Anglo-Norman invasion. They took part in the wars against the Danish invaders. The Annals note that in 1029 Macgawan O Regan, king of Breagh, defeated the forces of Sitric (the Danish king of Dublin) and captured his son Olaf who was released upon payment of a large ransom which included the famous sword of Carlus. The O Regans of Munster are of 11th century origin, being descended from Rioghan (of the Dalcass) who was son of Donncuan, brother to Brian Boru. The name is now widely prevalent in Eire. The Gaelic motto is translated "Mullach" (a placename) to Victory."

Ríoúʒaċ, -aiʒe, *a.,* impulsive, furious.

Ó néill, *Ó ɲéill.*

O Neill, O Neal, Neill, Neale, from the Gaelic *niall,* meaning a champion or military hero. This was anciently a very popular personal name. The surname was first established in the 9th century. Following are the principal houses of O Neill: (1) O Neill of Ulster descended from Neall Glundhuv (black knee) who was killed in battle with the Danes of Dublin in 919. These were the leaders of Cinel Eoghain (now Tyrone, Derry and part of Donegal) named from Eoghain, son of Niall of the Nine Hostages. They produced notable leaders and kings of Ulster from the 10th to the 17th century. Amongst them was Conn O Neill (created Earl of Tyrone by Henry III), Shane the Proud, Hugh, Sir Phelim and Owen Roe, all important in Irish history. Many of them attained to positions of importance with continental governments. (2) O Neill of Thomond, a Dalcassian house seated at Bunratty, Clare, and descended from Aodh Caoiv, king of Cashel (AD 571-601). Branches of this family were the O Nihills and Creaghs. (3) O Neill of Leinster, seated at Magh-da-chon (now Moyacomb) before the 11th century. Their territory lay across the boundary of Carlow and Wicklow. The Annals of the Four Masters record that one of their leaders was killed near Dublin in 1088 in a battle between forces of Munster and Leinster. The Coat of Arms is that of the principal O Neill family. Its Gaelic motto is translated "The red hand of Eire."

Niall, *g.* néill, *pl., id., m.,* a champion a soldier.

Lám Ḟeaʒʒ Deaṙʒ

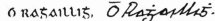

Ó Raġailliġ, *Ó Raġailliġ.*

O Reyly, O Riellie, O Realy, O Reely, O Reilly, O Reiley, O Rielly, O Realley, Reilly, Rielly, Really, Realy, Reely, Riley, from the Gaelic *ra(g)allac* or *railleac,* meaning unsettled or rakish or sportive. This surname was established by a family of the same stock as O Rourke, originally seated in Cavan, who gradually extended their domain (Breiney-O Reilly) until early in the 14th century, they controlled parts of Meath and Westmeath. They were active in church affairs and many of them were Primates of the ancient sea of Armagh. The motto is "By fortitude and prudence." Raılleaċ, -liġe, *a.,* rakish, sportive.

Ruaṫaṙḃaċ, *a.,* of restless disposition.

Ó Ruairc, *Ó Ruairc.*

O Ruaire, O Rowarke, O Rourke, O Roarke, O Rorke, Rourke, Rorke, from the Gaelic *ruaharac,* meaning restless or rushing. This surname was established in the 9th century by the chiefs of Ui Bruin Breifne, a powerful clan whose territory was basically co-extensive with the present counties of Leitrim and Cavan (Breiffney-O Rourke). The O Rourkes furnished three kings to the Ultonian throne in the 10th and 11th centuries. They offered sturdy resistance to English encroachment for several centuries and maintained independence until the 17th century. After the Cromwellian Massacres their leaders, being exiled, attained distinction in Europe, especially in Russia and Poland. A branch of the original house of O Rourke became affiliated with the Ui Maine at an early period and was seated in Galway. The Gaelic motto is translated "Uppermost" or "Victorious." Ruaṫanaċ, -aıġe, *a.,* rushing,

Ó Riaġaın,

Ó Maoılrıaġaın, *Ó Maoılrıaġaın.*

O Mulrigan, O Mulryan, O Mulrean, Múlryan, Mulroyan, Mulryne, Mulrine, Mulrain, O Ryan, Ryan, O Rian, from the Gaelic *ria(g)ain,* meaning a queen. It is therefore translated *of the queen* or *servant of the queen.* This surname originated with the leaders of the Ui Dhrona of Carlow in the 10th century. Their territory was co-extensive with the present Idrone barony in that county. A branch of this house assumed the name O Mulryan and in the 13th century settled in Uaithne-tire and Uaithne-cliach (now Owney and Owney-beg in Tipperary and Limerick respectively). Here they flourished until the 17th century confiscations resulting from the Cromwellian and Jacobite-Orange wars. The motto is "Death rather than disgrace." Rıaġán, *poet.* for ríoġán. Ríoġán, -ġna, *d.* -ġna, *f.,* a queen

Ó séaġḋa, Ō Séaġḋa.

O Shea, O Shee, Shea, Shee, from the Gaelic *sea(gd)a,* meaning learned, scientific, well informed. This surname originated with members of Corca Dhuibhne seated in west Kerry in the 13th century. A branch of this house became established in the city of Kilkenny about the end of the 14th century and another became affiliated with the Ui Fiachrach and located in Mayo at an early period but the family's greatest influence was in west Kerry where their descendants are still numerous. Séaġḋa, *indec. a.,* skilful, learned

Ó héaḋromáin, Ō ḡ Éaḋroṁáiḡ.

O Hederiman, Hederman, Hedderman, from the diminutive form of the Gaelic *edthrom,* which means not weighty, therefore *light,* also meaning frivolous. The records indicate that this surname originated in Fir Maigh (Fermoy) of the Ui Fidhgheinte of Cork and Limerick in the 10th century. The family divided in the 11th century. One branch remained in Limerick and the other appears to have followed the O Hehir into Clare. (See *O Brien's Rents* in Frost's History of Clare.) The name is found today in both counties. Thus it is obvious that this ancient name is in no way associated with the Germans from the Bavarian Palatinate who were brought to Limerick by the government of Queen Anne in 1709.

Éaḋrom, -ṛuime, *a.,* light (in weight), frivolous, fatuous. "touched"; nimble

Ó seacnasaiġ, Ō Seacġasaiġ.

O Shaughnessy, O Shoughnessy, O Shannessy, O Shanesy, Shaughnessy, Shannessy, from a variant of the Gaelic *sheacnach,* meaning elusive. This surname was established in the 12th century by the leaders of a branch of the Ui Fiachrach Aidhne who, early in the 13th century came into control of Cinel Aodh (now Kinlea) surrounding the present town of Gort in Galway. In 1533, Dermot O Shaughnessy, leader of his clan was knighted by Henry VIII and soon thereafter he transferred his clan lands to the English Crown and received them back with English title procedure. Thereafter the family attained an important place in national affairs until the 4th Sir Dermot joined the Confederation of Kilkenny and lost his property thru the Cromwellian confiscations. After the Restoration the family received back 2000 acres which was again forfeited in 1697 because they sided with the Stuarts in the Jacobite War. The last chief of this house, Colonel William O Shaughnessy died in France in 1744.

Seacnac, -aiġe, *a.,* avoiding, elusive

VIRTUTE ET FIDELITATE.

tuaṫal, -ail, *m.*, tyrant, a tactless act, rudeness

Ó Tuaṫail, Ō Tuaṫail.

O Toughill, O Touhill, O Twohill, O Tuale, O Towell, O Toole, Toughill, Tuohill, Twohill, Toohill, Tohall, Tohill, Towell, Toole, Toal, Toale, from *thua(t)hal,* meaning a rude, tactless or tyrannical person. This surname was first established in Leinster by the descendants of *Tua(t)hal,* son of Ughaire, king of Leinster who died A. D. 956. The O Tooles of Leinster were of the clan Ui Muireadhaigh in southern Kildare. In the Norman-English invasion they were defeated by the forces of Walter de Riddlesford and retreated to the Wicklow mountains where they operated from Ui Mail and Feara Cualann and, as allies of the O Byrne, waged war against the English for over four hundred years and maintained their independence until after the Treaty of Limerick in 1691. A branch of the O Tooles of Wicklow settled in Connaught after the Cromwellian wars and became numerous in Galway and Mayo. The motto is "By virtue and hospitality."

súil-aibiḋ (abaiḋ), sprightly-eyed, wide-awake

Ó Súileaḃáin, Ō Súileaḃáin.

O Sullivan, Sullivan, Sullevan, Soolivan, from a diminutive variant of the Gaelic compound *suil-abai(g)h,* meaning sprightly-eyed, or keen sighted. This surname was first established in Munster in the 10th century by a family, kindred to the MacCarthys, whose territory lay along the Suir. In 1192 the pressure of Anglo-Norman invasion forced them to retreat to the mountainous coast regions of Cork and Kerry where (at Kenmare and Bantry) they prospered and grew to be a powerful clan which later divided into important groups, namely: O Sullivan Mor, lord of Dunkerron; O Sullivan Beare, chief of Beare and Bantry; O Sullivan Maol. The estates of the O Sullivans were confiscated in the 17th century and many of their leaders took service with the governments of continental Europe. The Gaelic motto is translated "Success to the serious (or stately) hand."

FESTINA LENTE.

Pluincéid, Pluincéid.

Blounket, Plonket, Plunket, Plunkett, from the Norman-French Blanchet (diminutive of *blanc,* white, pale). This surname was that of an Anglo-Norman family which came to Ireland with the invasion. The Plunketts settled near Dublin and became a distinguished Norman-Irish family, attaining to the lordship of Killen, Fingall, Dunsanny and Louth. They managed to save most of their estates from the confiscation of the Cromwellian and Jacobite wars. The motto is "Make haste slowly."

mac póil, mac póil,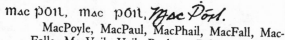

MacPoyle, MacPaul, MacPhail, MacFall, Mac-Falls, MacVail, Vail, Paulson, Polson, Powlson, MacPolin, MacPoland Polin, Poland, Powell, Powel, Poole, from the Gaelic form for *son of Paul* or *son of little Paul*. All forms of this name originated with an Ulster family of the 13th century. Branches of this family later were established in Connaught. The motto is "This is the virtue of my ancestors."   pól, -óil, *m.*, Paul.

mac póilín póil, *mac póilíg, póil.*

ve páor, *ve paor.*

Poer, Poor, Power, from the Norman *le Pover* (French "pauvre") i.e. poor. The founder of this Irish family came to Ireland with the first Anglo-Norman invasion and obtained from Strongbow a grant of conquered territory in Waterford. The descendants of the various branches of this family became numerous thruout Ireland.

ve priondargás. *ve priongoargás,*
ve priondoragás, *ve priongoragás.*

Prendergast, Prindergast, Pendergast, Pendergrass, Pender, Pinder, from Prendergast, a place name in Pembrokeshire, England. The founder of this family, Maurice de Prendergast, was a Norman knight who participated in the first Anglo-Norman invasion of Ireland. His descendants established important houses in Mayo, Galway, Limerick, Tipperary, Wexford and Kilkenny during the 13th to 17th centuries.

puirséil, *puirséil.*

Porcell, Purshell, Purcell, Purcill, Pursell, from the Norman *porcel*, a diminutive of the old French *porc*, therefore *little pig*, a nickname. This surname first appears in Irish history as that of a Norman family arriving in the 13th century. In the 14th century the family became established in Munster where the head of the house became Baron of Loughmoe and was seated near Thurles, Tipperary. The Purcells lost their possessions in the 16th and 17th century wars and their descendants were dispersed thruout Leinster and Munster. The motto is "I shall conquer or die."

ó cuain, Ó Cuaṁ.

O Cuayn, O Quane, Quan, Quann, Quane, Quaine, Coyne, Quaid, from the Gaelic *cuan,* a retiring person. This surname was established in Sligo by a branch of Ui Fiachrach which was seated at Ɖoonycoy in the 14th century. During the wars against Elizabeth's forces the family was dispersed and many of its members settled in Cork and Limerick. The motto is "I am resolved to look upward."

> Cúán, -áin, *pl. id., m.,* a quiet backward person.

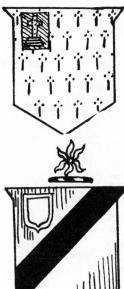

ó cuill, Ó Cuṁll.

O Quill, O Cwill, Quill, Quaile, from the Gaelic *coll,* which means hazel. This surname is of 10th century origin. The founding family seems to have been seated near Cahir, Tipperary. The leaders were bards and judges of ancient Thomond and many of them attained literary fame amongst their people. This name has sometimes been translated Woods because of its resemblance to *coill.* a wood. Coll, *g.* cuill, *m.,* the hazel tree; the Irish letter c

ó coiġliġ, Ó Coiġliġ.

O Cogly, O Cwigley, O Quigly, O Kegly, O Coigley, O Quigley, Cogley, Kegley, Quigley, Twigley, from the Gaelic *coigleac,* an escort or companion. This surname was established by 12th century leaders of a sept of the Ui Fiachrach which was located in Carra, Co. Mayo. After the invasion of Connaught by the Burkes this group was dispersed thruout Munster and Connaught.

> coiġliġim, *v. tr.,* I escort, accompany.

ó caoinḋealḃáin, Ó Caoinḋealḃáiġ.

O Guindelane, O Kennellan, O Kenolan, O Quinelane, Kindellan, Kennellan, Connellan, Kinlan, Kinlen, Kenlan, Conlan, Quinlivan, Quinlan, from the Gaelic *caoindeal(b)baun,* meaning fair white form. This surname was founded at Trim, County Meath in the 10th century by descendants of Caoindealbawn (died 925) who was directly descended from Laoghaire, (son of Niall of the Nine Hostages) an ard-ri of Eire during the lifetime of St. Patrick. The family became separated during the wars of invasion and many of them were driven to the maritime counties of the west.

> Caoin-ḋealḃ, *f.,* a fair form.
> Ɗán, -áine, *a.,* white.

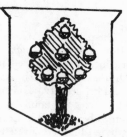

Ó CUIRC, *Ó Cuirc.*

O Cuirk, O Quirke, Quirk, Quirke, Querk, Kirk, from the Gaelic *cuirc,* meaning bushy-haired. This surname was established by the 12th century descendants of an ancient druid family of Munster. Before the invasion they were located in Muscraighe Cuirc in the present County Tipperary. After the invasion they became scattered thrus Cork, Kerry and Tipperary. cuirc, -uirc, a bushy tuft of hair

Ó REACTABRA, *Ó Reactabra,* Ó REACTAGÁIN, *Ó Reactagáin.*

O Raghtoury, Raftery, O Raghtagan, Roghtigan, Ractigan, Ratican, Ratigan, Rattigan, Rhategan, Rhatigan. Both forms of this name are from the Gaelic *reacthaire,* a law giver, administrator or steward. Both forms of this name were established in Roscommon in the 12th century by the descendants of an ancient druid family who were coarbs of St. Grellan (patron saint of Ui Maine) in the 5th century. The O Raghtigans became coarbs of the church property of St. Finnen and were seated at Clooncraff. comptroller

Reactaire, *g. id., pl.* -rí, *m.,* a lawgiver or administrator, a steward, manager,

Mac ζΙΟLLA RIABAIζ, *Mac ζiolla Riabaiζ,* Ó RIABAIζ, *Ó Riabaiζ.*

FORTI DIFFICILE ET FIDELI NIL

O Revoay, O Reogh, O Ria, O Ree, Reavey, Ravy, Reigh, Rea, Ray, McGillereogh, McCalreogh, McCalreaghe, McCallerie, MacGillreavy, MacGilrea, MacElreavy, MacIlravy, MacElreath, MacElwreath, MacIlwraith, MacIlrea, MacAreavy, MacArevy, Gallery, Callery, Killery, Milgray, Gray. Both forms of this name are from *giolla riabach,* which means the grey or brindled youth. This surname and its variant were established before the 14th century. The principal families were: (1) MacGillreavy, now Gallery of Clare, a Thomond family of McCarthy stock, who were at one time stewards to the O Briens of Thomond and held the Castle of Cragbrien at Clondagad. (2) MacGillreavy or O Reavy of Sligo, a family of Ui Fiachrach seated at Skreen. The name in its various forms is now prevalent thruout Eire. The name also is established in Gaelic Scotland where it is anglicized MacIlwraith. The motto is "To the brave and faithful nothing is difficult."

riabac, brindled

Ó MAOILDEIRζ, *Ó Maoildeirζ.*

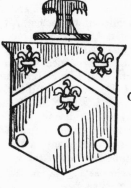

O Molgerge, Mulderg, Mulderrig, Reid, from *maol,* a chief, and *dearg,* red. Literally *from the red chief.* This surname appears to have been in existence among the Clans of Mayo, and Donegal as early as the 14th century. Reid and Ruthledge are translated forms of this name.

Dearg, -eirge, *a.,* red, bright red, crimson,

O RÍOȜBARDÁIN, *O Ríoȝбαrdαιȝ.*

O Riverdan, O Riourdane, O Reerdan, O Riordan, Riordan, Reardan, Reardon, from the diminutive of the Gaelic compound *rio(g)hbard,* meaning a royal poet. The chronicles indicate that this surname was first established in Offaly by the family of Rioghbardan, son of Cucoirne, lord of Ely O Carroll, who was killed at Aherlow in the year 1058. The O Riordans thrived in Offaly until the defeat of the O Carrolls when many of them settled in Kerry and Cork. The motto is "For God and country." Ríoȝóα, *indec. a.,* royal. Бαrdαmαιl, *-mlα, a.,* bardic.

O RODÁIN, *O Rodαιȝ.*

O Rodane, O Ruddane, O Rudden, Rodan, Roden, Rodin, Rodden, Rudden, Ruddon, Reddan, Reddin, from the Gaelic *rod(h),* meaning strength, heartiness. The Annals indicate that this name became established in the 13th century. The O Rodanes were numerous in Clare where they acted as stewards to the O Briens and McNamaras. Branches of the family were also located in Monaghan and Donegal. Roduιȝre, *p. a.,* hearty, lively.

O RODACÁin, *O Rodαcαιȝ,*
O RODAIȜ, *O Rodαιȝ.*

O Rodeghan, Rodaughan, Rudihan, Rudican, Redahan, Redehan, Redington, Reddington, O Roddy, O Ruddy, O Reddie, Roddy, Ruddy, Reddy. Both root forms of this name are from the Gaelic *rod(h)ach,* strong, hearty. This surname was originated in Connaught in the 12th century by a family of Ui Maine who were hereditary coarbs .of St. Caillin at Fenagh in County Leitrim and of other church property in Sligo and Galway. The motto is "Often for my king and always for my country."

mac RÉAmoinn, *mαc Réαmoιȝȝ.*

McRemon, MacRedmond, Redmond, all from the Gaelic form of a personal name introduced by the Normans and popular with the de Burgos or Burkes. Literally *son of Raymond.* This surname was established in the 14th century by a branch of the Norman-Irish Burkes of Connaught (See O Donovan in "O Kelly of Ui Maine"). The Redmonds were notable among the Irish of Norman descent who in later centuries fought so stubbornly for Irish liberty. Their names are frequently mentioned in connection with the Confederation of Kilkenny, the Cromwellian and Jacobite-Orange wars and (later) the Nationalist Cause. The motto is "Love conquers all."

Ó RUAĊAĠÁIN
Ó Ruaḋaġaiġ.

mac RUAIŎRÍ, Mac Ruaḋọrṫ.

McRury, McRoory, McRowry, MacRoary, Mac-Rory, MacArory, MacCrory, Rorison, Rogerson, Rogers, Rodgers, from *ru(d)hrach,* meaning holding possession or interests (also an ancient personal name, see note). This surname became established in Ulster in the 9th century by a family of Tellach Ainbhith who were once chiefs of Muinnter Birne in Tyrone and later erenaghs of church property at Ballynaskreen, Derry. A Scotch-Irish family descended from 14th century MacDonnell gallowglasses also assumed this name. The motto is "Always ready."

> Ruḋraċ, -aiġe, *a.,* holding possession by prescription, having vested interests
> Ruḋraiġe, *m.,* a personal name, Roger, Roderick.
> the Rudricians or true Ultonians (ṗíoṙ-ulaiḋ), descendants of Conall Ceaṙnaċ and ṗeaṙġuṙ mac Róiġ ; from them sprang many of the Irish Saints.

ɒe RÓISƚe, ɒe Róċċe.

Roche, Roache, from the Norman-French de la Roche, i.e. *of the rock.* This is an old Norman surname which came to Eire with the Norman-English invasion. There were at least three of this name among the first Norman adventurers. The Roches settled in Wexford, Cork and Limerick. In Cork they were established at Fermoy where the heads of the house in later centuries were Viscounts Fermoy. The Roches of Wexford soon became closely affiliated with the Gaelic clans. The Roches of Limerick City became substantial merchants but lost most of their property by Cromwellian confiscation because of their support of the Irish and Stuart Cause. The French motto is translated "My God is my rock."

Ó RUAĊÁIN, Ó Ruaḋáiṅ.

O Ruane, Ó Rowane, O Roan, Ruane, Rouane, Roane, Ruan, Roan, Roon, Rowan, Reẇan, Royan, Rogan, from the Gaelic *rua(d)an,* a red or a reddish-brown person. This surname was established in Connaught in the 11th century by a family of the Ui Maine a division of which later affiliated with the Ui Fiachrach. The O Ruanes became a noted ecclesiastical family of Mayo and Galway and at least six of the name were bishops in the different dioceses of Connaught between the 12th and 14th centuries. In Galway the name has sometimes been anglicized Ryan but this is not to be confused with the O Ryans discussed elsewhere in this book.

> Ruaḋán, -áin, *pl. id., m.,* a red or reddish-brown person, animal or thing ; redness.

O RIȵȵ, Ō Riȵȵ.

O Rinne, O Ring, Rinn, Rynn, Ring, Reen, Wrynn, Wren, Wrenn, from *reann,* a star or constellation. This surname was first assumed in the 12th century by members of the Ui Macaille who were seated in the district now known as the barony of Imokilly in the County Cork. A branch of this family later became established in Roscommon and their descendants became numerous in Connaught.

> Reann, *g.* -a and ꞁinne; *pl.* -a, -nᴄa, *f.* (*old neut.*), a star, a constellation

O RÓȵáiȵ, Ō Rōȵáiȵ.

O Ronane, O Ronayne, Ronane, Ronayne, Ronan, from the diminutive of *ron,* a seal. Prior to the Norman English invasion this surname was well established in different Irish clans. The more important groups of the name are here mentioned. (1) O Ronan of Connaught, members of the Ui Fiachrach seated in Mayo. (2) O Ronan of Munster, a brehon family of Corca Laoidhe. (3) O Ronan of Granard, chiefs of Cairbre Gabhra. (4) O Ronan of Dublin, hereditary erenaghs of Clondalkin. The motto is "Strong and faithful."

> Rón, -óin, *pl.* -óinᴄe, -ónᴄa, *m.,* a seal, a sea-calf.

Ruiséiꞁ, Ruiséiꞁ.

Rushell, Rosel, Rossell, Russell, from the diminutive of the Norman-French *rous* i.e. red or red-haired. The founders of this Norman-Irish family were followers of Sir John de Courcy who originally settled in Down but whose descendants later became numerous thruout all four provinces. The motto is "What will be, will be."

O Ruaȵaiᴅ, Ō Ruaȵaiᴅ, O Ruaȵaᴅa, Ō Ruaȵaᴅa.

O Rownoe, O Roney, Rooney, Rowney, Roney, from the Gaelic *ruanai(d)h,* strong, mighty. This surname was first established in Ulster in the 9th century by a bardic family. Altho the name was found in many parts of Ireland before the 14th century the origin seems to have been in the powerful Oirghialla. The Annals record that Ceallach O Rooney was chief poet and an officer of the national government early in the 11th century and died in 1079.

> Ruaȵaiᴅ, -e, *a.,* strong, mighty.

Ó SCOLAIÒE. *Ó Scolaiòe.*

O Scollee, O Scully, Scully, Skelly, Scallon, Scally, from the Gaelic *sgolai(d)he,* meaning a schoolman. This surname was estabished in Westmeath in the 10th century by a family having a zone of influence around West Delvin. They were forced out by pressure from the Norman-English in the 12th century and later became wardens of the church property of St. Ruadhan in Tipperary. There they remained until the 15th century after which they scattered thru Munster and Leinster.

> Scolaiòe, *g. id., m.,* a learner, a scholar
> a schoolboy, a schoolman

Ó scannail, *Ó Scannail,*
ó scannláin, *Ó Scannláin.*

O Scandall, O Scannill, O Scannell, Scannell, O Scanlaine, O Scanlan, O Scandlon, Scanlan, Scanlon, Scandlon. Both forms are from the Gaelic word meaning scandal or calumny. The surname and its variants appear in the Annals as originating with a Sligo family of the Ui Cairbre, descended from Niall of the Nine Hostages and flourishing at Carbury in the 12th century. In the following century one of their number Maolpadraig O Scannell was elevated from Bishop of Raphoe to Primate of Armagh. Branches of this family appear to have become erenaghs of Cloyne (Cork) and Devenish (Fermanagh) at an early date. Another family with the diminutive form of this name became part of the Ui Fiachrach thru affiliation with the O Shaughnessys of Galway. The name is now common in Cork, Galway, Kerry, Limerick and Clare. The Gaelic motto is translated "Saint Columkille and the Angel."

> Scannal, -ail, *pl. id., m.,* a scandal,
> scandal, reproach, blasphemy, calumny.

Ó seasnáin, *Ó Seasnáin.*

O Sesnane, O Shesnan, Shasnan, Sexton, from the Gaelic *s(h)easnawn,* a bodyguard. This surname was established in Clare in the 11th century by a Dalcassian family serving with the household troops of the O Brien kings of Thomond. In the 15th century members of the family migrated to Ulster and in the 16th century the anglicized form Sexton became common altho the original Gaelic form of the name is still commonly used by the bilingual people of Clare and Galway.

> Seasnán, -áin, *pl. id., m.,* a body-guard.

> Seasuisim, *vl.* seas, seasam, *imper.* seas,
> seasaim, -ruis, *pret.* 3 *s.,* seas, -ruis,
> -saim, *v. tr.* and *intr.,* I stand, take my
> stand, halt, stop, last, endure, maintain,
> sustain

O SAORAIDE, Ó Saopajde.

O Seyry, O Serie, Seerey, Seery, Freeman, Earner, O Shrue, O Shirie, O Shyry, from the Gaelic *saor(h)ui(d)he,* meaning free or delivered. It appears from the chronicles of Connaught that this surname existed in the Ui Fiachrach Aidhne and other clans as early as the 12th century. The name is now common in Mayo and Galway. The Gaelic motto is translated "A rough and good man" or "A rough man and a good one."

> SAORAIM, -RAÓ, *v. tr.,* I save, free, deliver, rescue, redeem, exempt, acquit,

O SEANACÁIN, Ó Seagacáiy.

O Sheanaghaine, O Shanahan, Shanaghan, Shanahan, Shanihan, Shanan, from the diminutive form of the Gaelic *sheanach,* old (wise). This surname was founded in Thomond in the 11th century by leaders of the Dalcassian sept Ui Ronghaile. Their descendants are still numerous in Clare altho many of them migrated to Waterford in 1318 under pressure from the O Briens and MacNamaras. The motto is "Neither depressed nor elated."

> SEANAÓ, *m.,* act of growing old
> SEAn, RINE. *pl.* -A, *a.,* old, aged.

MAC SEANLAOIC, Mac Seagaoic.

McShanlie, McShanly, MacShanley, Shanley, McGanley, Ganley, Ganly, from the Gaelic *shan,* old and *laoch,* a hero. This surname was established in Connaught in the 12th century by members of Corca Achlann seated in Roscommon and Leitrim. It would appear that they were also affiliates of Ui Fiachrach. The motto is "By God's favor." LAOCAR, -AIR, *m.,* heroism

O SEANAIS, Ó Seagais,
O SEANÁIN, Ó Seagáis.

O Shanna, O Shanny, Shannagh, Shanny, O Shenane, O Shanan, O Shennan, O Shannon, Shanan, Shanon, Shannon, O Sheny, O Sunny, Shunny, Shinagh, Shinnick, Shinnock, Shinwick, Seeny, Fox, from derivatives of *shan,* old or ancient. This surname is one of the oldest of Connaught names. Various historical documents extant show that the name in its different forms was common in clans of Kerry, Clare, Galway and Mayo before the 10th century, also in Corca Laoighdhe (S.W. Cork). The name has sometimes been translated *Fox* because of the similarity of one of its variants to the Gaelic word for fox.

> SEAn, *g.* RIn, *pl. id., m.,* an old person, an ancestor, an elder, an ancient

Ó síoⱱA, Ō SjóⱱA.

O Shydie, Sheedy, Silk, from the Gaelic *shiod(h)a,* a silk or fine raiment. The chronicles of Galway record this surname in the 12th century. It was there established by members of septs of Ui Fiachrach Aidhne and Ui Maine.

síoⱱA, *g. id., pl.* -Aí, *m.,* silk.

Ó síoⱱacáin, Ō Sjóⱱcáĩŋ.

O Shieghane, O Shehane, O Sheehan, O Sheahan, Sheehan, Sheahan, Sheean, Sheen, Shean, from *sheo(d)hac,* peaceful. This surname appears to have originated in the early 11th century with a family, followers of O Kelly of Ui Maine, whose descendants are still numerous in Galway. A branch of this family (fostered into Dalcass in an alliance of the O Kelly and the O Briens of Thomond) spread from Clare thru Cork, Kerry and Limerick. síoⱱac, -AiⵉE, *a.,* peaceable, calm. at peace with

mac sícíⵉ, Mac Sjíⵉ.

McShihy, McShiehie, McShee, MacSheehy, Sheehy, from a variant of the Gaelic *seo(d)hach,* peaceful. This surname was first established in Ireland by a branch of the MacDonnells of Scotland (from Shi(t)heach, great-grandson of Doh(m)naill) who came to Ireland early in the 14th century as MacDonnell gallowglasses. The name first appears in Irish Annals in connection with a civil war between the O Connor rulers of Connaught in 1367. It is also recorded that ·the MacSheehys came into Munster in 1420 as constables to the Earl of Desmond and settled in Limerick, building their castle at Lisnacolla.

síⵉ, *gs.* of ŗíoⵉ as *a.,* peaceful ; *al.* for ŗíⱱe, *gs.* of ŗíoⱱ

Ó siŗiⱱeáin, Ō Sŗiⱱeáĩŋ.

O Shiridane, O Sheridane, Sheridan, Sherridan, from the diminutive of the Gaelic *shiradh,* meaning investigating, seeking or reconnoitring. This surname was first established in Longford by a family who were custodians of church property (erenaghs) of Granard prior to the 14th century. In the 15th century the house appears to have moved to Cavan and in the 16th century they became part of clan O Reilly. In the next two centuries the house of O Sheridan came to prominence in the fields of politics, law and art.

siŗim (ŗíŗim), *vls.* ŗiŗeáⱱ, ŗúŗ, *v. tr.,* I seek. look for investigate, reconnoitre.

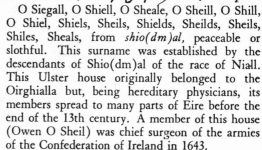

O SIAȜAIL O SIAȮAIL, Ó Sȝaȝaȝl, Ó SȝaȮaȝl.

O Siegall, O Shiell, O Sheale, O Sheill, O Shill, O Shiel, Shiels, Sheils, Shields, Sheilds, Sheils, Shiles, Sheals, from *shio(dm)al,* peaceable or slothful. This surname was established by the descendants of Shio(dm)al of the race of Niall. This Ulster house originally belonged to the Oirghialla but, being hereditary physicians, its members spread to many parts of Eire before the end of the 13th century. A member of this house (Owen O Sheil) was chief surgeon of the armies of the Confederation of Ireland in 1643.

SíoȮaṁaıl, -ṁla, *a.,* peaceable. peaceful

O SLATRA Ó Slatpa,
O SLATARRA. Ó Slatappa.

O Slattra, O Slattery, Slattery, from the Gaelic *slathra,* strong, robust, bold. This surname originated in Thomond in the 12th century with members of the Dalcass and were located at Ballyslattery in Clare. In the 16th and 17th centuries they were scattered thru Munster but their descendants are still most numerous in east Clare.

Slatpa, *a.,* robust (*O'R.*) ; -tappa, *id.* (*ib.*).

O SLEIȮÍN Ó Sléȝḃúȝ.

O Slevine, O Slevan, Slevin, Sleavin, Sleevin, Slevan, Slavin, Slamon, from the diminutive form of the Gaelic *sliav,* a mountain. This surname was first established in the 7th century by a branch of Cinel Eoghain. Giolla Co(mg)aill O Sleivin was chief bard of Ulster in the reign of Malachy, King of Ireland before Brian Boru. The Gaelic motto is translated "Uppermost."

SlıaḃȮa, *indec. a.,* mountainous.

O SLUAȜAȮAIȜ ÓSluaȝaȮaıȝ,
O SLUAȜAȮÁIN ÓSluaȝaȮáıȝ.

O Slowey, Slowey, Sloey, Sloy, A Sloan, Sloane, Sloan, Slown, Slone, Sloyan, Sloyne, from *sluagagh;* meaning of hosts, gathering together for raiding or military purposes. Both forms of this surname were first established in Roscommon in the latter part of the 9th century by a family of bards and brehons who were of sufficient importance to be mentioned in the Annals of the Four Masters wherein we read that Maolpadraig O Slowey, a philosopher of national importance, died in 1015. Descendants of the original houses of this name spread thruout Ulster and Connaught at an early date. However, the Sloanes of Antrim and Down seem to be from a Scottish family with the same root form of Gaelic name.

SluaȝaȮ, *g.* -aıȮ, *m.,* a hosting, a levee or mobilisation, a military expedition or raid

O SAṁRAiṫ, Ō Saiṁraiṫ.

O Sawrie, O Sawra, Summers, Sommers, Somers, from *sa(m)radh*, summer. This surname was first established in Leinster. Later a division of the family settled in Wexford whence they spread into Carlow, Limerick and Waterford (see McGovern).

ᵳaṁᵳaiṫ, summer

O spealáin, Ō Speálain.

O Spallane, O Spillane, O Spollane, Spalane, Spellane, Spillane, Spollane, Spollan, Splane, Splaine, Smallen, Smollan, Smullen, Spelman, Spellman, from *speallain,* a chip or shaving. This surname was established in the 12th century by a family of the Ui Fiachrach located at Cullen in Sligo. Members of this family later became leaders of a sept (Ui Luighdheach) in Tipperary.

> Speaᴌan, -áin, *pl. id., m.,* a shaving, a chip.
> Speaᴌ, -eiᴌe, *d.* -eiᴌ, *pl.* -ᴀ, -ᴄᴀ, *f.,* a scythe

ọ ᵳuᴀoᴀ, Ō ᵳuᴀoᴀ.

O Foodie, O Foedy, O Foody, Foody, Foudy, Foddy, and translated Swift and Speed from the Gaelic *fuadh,* haste. This surname is recorded as having been founded by a 12th century family of the Ui Fiachrach which was located in the barony of Carra, Mayo. The motto is "Make haste slowly."

ᵳuᴀo, *m.,* haste.

O suᴀiᴿo, Ō Suaiᵳᵳo.
O suᴀiᴿᴄ, Ō Suaiᵳᵳᴄ.

O Sworde, O Swerte, Sword, Seward, Swords, from the Gaelic *suairce,* meaning pleasantness or graciousness. This surname was established toward the end of the 9th century by leaders of a sept in Offaly. The Annals of the Four Masters indicate that they were of consequence at an early date by the following notation: "Eithne, daughter of the O Suard, abbess of Kildare, died 1016." The motto is "Virtue tried flourishes."

> Suᴀiᴿce, *g. id., f.,* pleasantness, graciousness, wit, drollery.

FORTE ET FIDELE.

⊤ɑlƀóıƉ *⊤ɑlƀóρƉ.*

Talebot, Talbote, Talbot, from Talebot, a Norman personal name. This Norman-Irish family was established by the descendants of Richard Talbot who came to Ireland in the reign of Henry II and obtained the lordship of Malahide, Co. Dublin which had been retained in the line of his descendants to the present time. The French motto is translated "Strong and faithful."

Ó ⊤ɑɩ⊤lɩʒ *Ó ⊤ɑι⊤lιʒ.*
Ó ⊤ɑɩl⊤ɩʒ *Ó ⊤ɑρ⊤ɑιʒ.*

O Talheighe, Tally, Tully, Tilly, O Talty, Talty, Taulty, from the Gaelic *taithleach,* peaceful, quiet. The root surname and its variant originated with the 9th century chiefs of Ui Laoghaire in Tyrone whose descendants became hereditary trustees of church estates (erenaghs), especially in Fermanagh. The O Taltys of Clare are a branch of this family. The Gaelic motto is translated "The red hand of Eire."

⊤ɑι⊤leɑċ, *a.,* quiet, peaceable.

Ó ⊤ɩʒeɑρnɑɩʒ *Ó ⊤ɩʒeɑρɲɑɩʒ.*

O Tierny, O Tearney, O Tierney, Tierney, Terney, Tiernan, Ford, from *thi(g)earnach,* lordly. This surname was established before the 13th century. The following are the chief families: O Tierney of Ulster, a branch of Cinel Eoghain seated at Fearnmaigh, Donegal; O Tierney of Westmeath, a branch of the Ui Neill; O Tierney of Clare and Tipperary, a branch of the Westmeath family.

⊤ɩʒeɑρnɑ, *g. id. (smt. -n), pl. -i, m.,* a lord, a master, a proprietor

Ó ⊤ɩʒeɑρnáɩn *Ó ⊤ɩʒeɑρɲáιɲ.*

O Ternane, O Tiernan, Tiernan, Ternan, from the diminutive of the Gaelic *thierna,* (a lord). This surname was established in the 11th century. It was first used by a distinguished family of the Ui Fiachrach whose domain was once located at Carra. They later became numerous in Connaught.

⊤ɩʒeɑρnɑṁɑɩl, *-ṁlɑ, a.,* imperious, lordly, haughty.

⊤ɩʒeɑρnɑṁlɑċ⊤, *-ɑ, f.,* lordliness, lordship,

mac τaιυϛ mac τaιυϛ, *Mac Taidȝ, Mac Taidȝ.*

MacTeigue, MacTigue, MacTeague, MacTague, Montague, Teige, Teigue, Teague, Tague, Tigue, Tighe, MacHeig, MacKeige, MacAig, MacHaig, MacCaig, MacCaigue, MacKaige, MacKague, MacKage, MacKaigue, MacKeag, MacKeague, Keag, Keague, from *tha(d)g*, (a poet or philosopher). This has always been a popular personal name in western Ireland where it was first so used by the O Kellys of Ui Maine in which the MacTeiges originated and of which they founded the sept, Muintear Siorthachain. Their descendants became numerous in. Connaught and Munster. The motto is "Let us neither fear nor wish for the last day." τaυϛ, -aιυϛ, *m.*, a poet (*Dav.*), personal name Teig, Teague or Thady, Tady (=Thaddeus) and equated with Timothy

mac an τιompanaιϛ *Mac an Tiompanaiȝ.*

McItempany, McTympane, McTempane, MacAtimney, MacAtimeny, MacAtamney, MacAtaminey, MacTimney, MacTamney, Timpany, Tympany, Tymmany, Timony, Tamney, Tempeny, Tenpeny, Toompane, Tumpany, from the Gaelic *thiompanach,* (noisy). This surname originated in Ulster. The records indicate that its bearers were numerous in Tyrone where they served as kern of the army of the O Neills. The Gaelic motto is "Uppermost."

τιompanaċ, -aιϛe, *a.*, relating to a tympanum, noisy, disorderly, troubled

τοιϐιn *Toibȝ.*

Tobine, Tobyn, Tobin, from the Norman *de St Aubyn* (of St. Aubyn) a city of Brittany. This surname came to Ireland with the Norman-English invasion. The Tobins established themselves thruout Munster, the family seat being in Tipperary where the head of the house was known as Baron Comsey.

ó τuama *Ó Tuama.*

O Twomey, O Toomey, Twomey, Toomey, Twoomey, Tuomy, Towmey, from *thuam,* (a sound). This surname originated with a Dalcassian family of hereditary bards. The chronicles and traditions of Munster attest to their importance in their particular field. Their descendants are numerous in Cork.

τuaιm, -ama, and -e, *f.*, a sound.

ó τυατaις, *Ó Τυατaις.*

O Twohy, O Towie, Twohy, Twoohy, Tuohy, Touhy, Toohy, Tuhy, Tooey, Towey from the Gaelic *thuathac,* (sturdy). This surname was first used in the 11th century by a family of Ui Maine, seated at Aughrim in Galway and constituting a sept of O Maddens' clan (see clans). By the first of the 17th century the O Tuohys were scattered thru all the provinces.

τυατač, -aιše, *a.,* rustic, sturdy.

ó cuinn, *Ó Cuinn.*

O Quyn, O Quine, O Quin, Quin, Quinn, Queen, from the Gaelic *conn,* (sense or reason). This surname was established in various Gaelic clans beginning with the 9th century. The following are the more important of the families: O Quin of Thomond, leaders of Muintear Ifearnain, a sept of the Dal Cass. (These were seated at Inchiquin and in the 10th century their lands were coterminus with the present Corofin, Clare.) O Quin of Antrim, chiefs of Siol Cathasaigh whose leader, Congalach, was slain by the Norman-English in 1218. O Quin of Mayo, members of Ui Fiachrach and leaders of clan Cluain at Castlebar (at the end of the 11th century they separated from Ui Fiachrach, joined Siol Muireadhaigh and became followers of McDermott of Moyburg); O Quinn of Longford, leaders of Muinntear Ciollagain of Conmaicne who were replaced by the O Farrells in the 14th century. The motto is "I am resolved to look upward."

Conn-, -conn, sense.

ó τreαδaιr, *Ó Τreαδaιr.*

O Trevir, O Trover, Treyor, Trower, Trevors, Travors, Travers, from the Gaelic *threa(b)ar,* (prudent). This surname was established by a branch of the MacClancy. The O Trevirs were hereditary erenaghs of Killagra in Leitrim and later became an important ecclesiastical family in that county. The motto is "Wounds are life to me." τreαδar, *gsf.,* -aιre, τreιδιre, *a.,* industrious, prudent, solvent

δreατnač, *δreατnač.*

Brathnagh, Brethnagh, Brehnagh, Brennagh, Brannagh, Walsh, Walshe, from the Gaelic *Breathnac,* (a Welshman). This name was generally applied by the native Irish to all Norman-English invaders coming to Ireland from Wales. It was generally translated Walsh or Welsh which is now a common name thruout Ireland.

δreατnač, -aιše, *a.,* Welsh; *sm.,* a Welshman, a Briton; *al.* δreατnač.

Mac CORMAIC. *Mac Copmaic.*

McCormick, MacCormac, MacCormack, Mac-Cormick, Cormac, Cormick, Cormack, from the Gaelic *cuirmach* charioteerThis surname was evidently established more or less permanently in Munster before the 9th century by some of the descendants of Cormac Cas, son of Olliol Ollum, King of Munster A. D. 177 and Sabia, daughter of Con of the Hundred Battles, Ard-Ri of Ireland A. D. 148. The Geneological Tracts of Thordealbach O Raithbhealtaigh indicate that members of this group were anciently chieftains of Conmaicne Duine Moir. The foundation of the name was popular as a personal name even at the dawn of Irish history as is evidenced by its frequent appearance in all the ancient manuscripts.

Cap̃b, *m.,* a chariot.
Mac, *g.* mic, a son, a boy.

Ó TREASAIg, *Ó Cpeapaiξ.*

O Trassy, O Tressy, O Trasey, Trassy, Tressy, Tracy, Tracey, Treacy, from the Gaelic *threassach,* (embattled). This surname was first established in Galway in the 12th century by a family of Siol Anmchadha (Ui Maine). Another family of the name was seated at Slievemargy in Leix. The motto is "Brave in the cause of virtue."

Cpeapac, -aiξe, *a.,* embattled

Mac an BÁIRD, *Mac an báppd.*

MacAward, MacWard, Ward, from Mac an bard, i.e. son of the bard. This surname was adopted in Galway in the 11th century by hereditary bards to the O Kellys of Ui Maine. Other families of the name were: MacWard of Orgialla and MacAward of Tirconnell, bards to the O Donnells. The motto is "Salvation thru the cross."

báпṽ, -áiṗṽ, *pl. id.,* *m.,* a poet, a bard

Ó vanáin, *Ó banáiɲ.*

O Banane, O Bannan, O Bynnan, Banane, Banan, Bannan, Bannon, Banim, O Banion, White, Whyte, from the Gaelic *bawnan,* literally: little white one, a haunter of battlefields. This surname was first established by an Offaly family, followers of the O Carrolls. Branches of the parent family later settled in Connaught and Ulster especially in Mayo and Fermanagh.

bánáin, -áin, -áná, *m.,* a preternatural being haunting battlefields, *etc.*

Ó ꝼíonnmacáin, *Ō ꝼroggymacáing.*

Finnucane, Finucane, from the Gaelic ꝼíonnmacán *tair little son*
The surname first appears in the Annals as that of followers of MacMahon
of Clare (members of Dalcass) founded by Mahon, son of Murthagh Mor
O Brien, King of Ireland from 1094 to 1119. Their sept was Corca Baiscin,
occupying the present baronies of Moyarta and Clonderlaw.

mac conſaíoín, *Mac Cogrᴣroᴣfg.*

Considine, son of **Constantine**, a Clare family of the Dalcass deriving
its descent from the O Brien Kings.

mac nuᴁoᴁo, *Mac Nuᴁoᴁo.*
mac nuᴁoᴁt, *Mac Guᴁoᴁt*
MacNutt, Noud, Nowd, son of nuᴁoᴁ, the name of a sea-divinity   See
                                                                   Noonan

Heraldic Color Indications.

Gold   Silver   Red   Blue   Green   Purple   Black

ABBREVIATIONS

a., adj., adjective; *acc.,* accusative; *ad.,* adverb; *art.,* article; *coll.,* collective; *comp.,*
comparative; *conj.,* conjunctions; *corr.,* corrupt; *d.,* dative; *def.,* definite, defective;
dep., dependent, deponent; *dim.,* diminutive; *disturb.,* distributive; *dpl.,* dative
plural; *ds.,* Decies of Munster; *f.,* feminine; *fig.,* figuratively; *fut.,* future; *g.,* genitive;
gs., genitive singular; *gsf.,* genitive singular feminine; *imper.,* imperative; *impers.,*
impersonal; *indef.,* indefinite; *indic.,* indicative; *intens.,* intensive; *interj.,* inter-
jection; *intr.,* intransitive; *irreg.,* irregular; *m.,* masculine; *met.,* metaphorically; *mg.,*
meaning; *n.,* nominative; *neg.,* negative; *neut.,* neuter; *nom.* nominative; *num.,*
numeral; *obs.,* obsolete; *pass.,* passive; *perf.,* perfect; *pers.,* person, personal; *phr.,*
phrase; *pl.,* plural; *poet.* poetical, poetry; *poss.,* possessive; *pref.,* prefix; *prep.,* prepo-
sition; *prn., pr.,* pronoun, pronominal; *prov.,* proverb, provincial; *refl.,* reflex, reflexive;
rel., relative; *sf.* substantive feminine; *sg.,* singular; *sing.,* singular; *sl.,* slang; *sm.,*
substantive masculine; *smt.,* sometimes; *subj.,* subjunctive, subject; *sub., subst.,* substantive; *suff.,* suffix; *v., vb.,* verb; *var.,* variant; *vars.,* variants; *vl.,* verbal; *voc.,*
vocative.

INDEX OF NAMES BY PAGE

Loughlen, 104. Loughlin, 85, 104. Loughnan, 71. Loughnane, 71. Loughran, 72. Loughrane, 72. Loughren, 72. Loughrey, 72. Loughry, 72. Lyhan, 70. Lyhane, 70. Lyman, 72. Lynan, 72. Lynam, 72. Lynch, 71. Lynchahaun, 71. Lynchahan, 71. Lynchehan, 71. Lynchy, 71. Lyne, 68. Lyneham, 72. Lynham, 72. Lyons, 68, 70. Lysaght, 74. Lysat, 74.

Macabe, 77. Macbride, 50. Machelbreed, 50. Macingill, 81. Mackey, 73. Macleavy, 36. Macmorris, 44. Macmurray, 52. Madden, 73. Maddigan, 73. Madigan, 73. Magahan, 48, 81. Magaheran, 48. Magahern, 48. Magann, 48. Magauran, 74. Magaurn, 74. Magawran, 74. Mageachrane, 48. Mageahan, 81. Magean, 81. Magee, 81. Mageehan, 81. Magennis, 74. Magenor, 50. Magennure, 50. Mageraghty, 49. Magher, 75. Magill, 81. Maginn, 74. Maginess, 74. Maginnoire, 50. Maglen, 83. Maglinne, 83. Magloan, 83. Magloin, 83. Maglone, 83. Maglyne, 83. Magoveran, 74. Magovern, 74. Magowan, 84. Magragh, 79. Magrath, 79. Magraw, 79. Magreavy, 84. Magreevy, 84. Magueen, 89. Maguier, 84. Maguiness, 74. Maguinness, 74. Maguire, 84. Magurn, 74. Maharry, 48. Maher, 75. Mahon, 75, 86. Mahony, 75, 86. Malady, 90. Mallaghan, 91. Mallan, 75. Mallen, 75. Malley, 102. Malone, 76, 83. Malowny, 76. Manahan, 92. Manally, 87. Mangan, 76. Mangin, 76. Manion, 76. Mannassas, 86. Mannice, 1. Mannight, 88. Mannin, 76. Manning, 76. Mannion, 76. Manus, 86. Many, 76. Mara, 101. Markahan, 77. Markan, 77. Markham, 77. Marrinan, 105. Maughan, 75, 92. Meade, 90. Meagh, 90. Meagher, 75. Mealley, 102. Meally, 102. Meany, 76, 92. Meara, 101. Meath, 87. Mee, 87. Meelderry, 94. Meehan, 90. Meeny, 92. Meghan, 48, 81. Meggin, 74. Meginniss, 74. Megrath, 79. Megraw, 79. Melane, 87. Meldon, 90. Meleady, 90. Meledy, 90. Melia, 102. Melican, 91. Mellan, 75. Melledy, 90. Mellon, 75. Melly, 102. Melody, 90. Meloy, 75. Melvenny, 96. Melville, 91. Melvin, 91. Melroy, 95. Menaght, 88. Menautt, 88. Miache, 90. Miagh, 90. Michail, 91. Millan, 87. Millane, 87. Millican, 91. Milligan, 91. Milligen, 91. Milliken, 91. Millikin, 91. Milgray, 112. Milroy, 95. Minett, 88. Minnerk, 82. Minnish, 1. Minnitt, 88. Mitchell, 91. Moan, 92. Moen, 92. Moghan, 92. Mohan, 92. Mollan, 87. Molloy, 75. Molohan, 91. Maloney, 76. Molony, 76. Molowny, 76. Molvin, 91. Monaghan, 92. Monahan, 92. Mongan, 76. Mongon, 76. Money, 92. Monk, 92. Monks, 92. Montauge, 122. Moohan, 92. Moon, 92. Mooney, 92. Moore, 93. Morahan, 93. Moran, 92. Morchan, 93. More, 93. Morey, 93. Morgan, 93. Moriarty, 93. Morissy, 94. Morkan, 93. Morkin, 93. Mornan, 105. Moroney, 94. Morooney, 94. Morphy, 96. Morran, 93. Morrin, 93. Morris, 44, 94. Morrissey, 94. Morrison, 44, 94. Morrissy, 94. Morrogh, 86. Morrough, 86. Morrow, 86. Morrowson, 86. Moughan, 92. Mowen, 92. Moylan, 87. Mulcahy, 94. Mulconry, 20. Muldarry, 94. Mulderg, 112. Mulderrig, 112. Mulderry, 94. Muldon, 90. Muldoon, 90. Muldooney, 76. Muldowney, 76. Muldowny, 76. Mulgan, 91. Mulhall, 95. Mulhane, 87. Mulheran, 95. Mulhern, 95. Mulherrin, 95. Mulherron, 95. Mulkearn, 95. Mulkearns, 95. Mulkeeran, 95. Mulkern, 95. Mulkerns, 95. Mulkerrin, 95. Mulkieran, 95. Mullagan, 91. Mullan, 87. Mullane, 87. Mullaney, 95. Mullally, 68. Mullaly, 68. Mullany, 95. Mulleady, 90. Mullen, 75, 87. Mulligan, 91. Mullin, 87. Mullins, 87. Mullin, 87. Mullon, 87. Mulloy, 75. Mullowney, 76. Mulveen, 91. Mulrain, 107. Mulrine, 107. Mulroe, 95. Mulrony, 94. Mulrooney, 94. Mulrow, 95. Mulroy, 95. Mulroyan, 107. Mulryan, 107. Mulryne, 107. Mulry, 95. Mulvagh, 96. Mulvanny, 96. Mulvany, 96. Mulveen, 91. Mulvenna, 96. Mulvenny, 96. Mulvey, 96. Mulvihill, 91. Mulvin, 91. Murchan, 93. Murchoe, 96. Murdock, 79. Murdough, 79. Murdow, 79. Murdy, 79. Murkin, 93. Murnain, 105. Murnan, 105. Murnane, 105. Murphy, 96. Murray, 52, 96. Murrihy, 96. Murrooney, 94. Murrough, 86. Murrow, 86. Murry, 52, 96. Murt, 79. Murta, 79. Murtagh, 93. Murtaugh, 79, 93. Murtha, 79. Myagh, 90. Mac Abee, 89. Mac Agill, 81. Mac Aig, 122. Mac Agowne, 84. Mac Alea, 36. Mac Alean, 85. Mac Alester, 77. Mac Aleavy, 36. Mac Alister, 77. Mac Allen, 85. Mac Aline, 85. Mac Alline, 85. Mac Allion, 85. Mac Allister, 77. Mac Allon, 85. Mac Aloon, 83. Mac Aloone, 83. Mac Alroy, 52. Mac Anally, 87. Mac Anern, 82. Mac Anerney, 82. Mac Anlevy, 35. Mac Ann, 78. Mac Anulty, 88. Mac Areavy, 112. Mac Aree, 83. Mac Arevy, 112. Mac Arory, 114. Mac Arthy, 81. Mac Ataminey, 122. Mac Atamney, 122. Mac Atimeny, 122. Mac Atimney, 122. Mac Auley, 73. Mac Auliffe, 73. Mac Aveigh, 89. Mac Avey, 89. Mac Avoy, 78. Mac Award, 124.

Mac Brearty, 79. Mac Briarty, 79. Mac Bride, 50. Mac Brody, 8.

Mac Cabe, 77. Mac Caffarky, 81. Mac Cafferchie, 81. Mac Cafferkie, 81. Mac Cafferty, 81. Mac Cafiry, 81. Mac Cagherty, 81. Mac Caharty, 81. Mac Caherty, 81. Mac Caig, 122. Mac Caigue, 122. Mac Call, 15. Mac Callister, 77. Mac Cann, 78. Mac Canny, 78. Mac Carha, 81. Mac Carhie, 81. Mac Carhig, 81. Mac Carnon, 66. Mac Carrie, 83. Mac Cartan, 78. Mac Carten, 78. Mac Carthy, 81. Mac Cartie, 81. Mac Cartin, 78. Mac Carton, 78. Mac Carty, 81. Mac Cashin, 14. Mac Caugherty, 81. Mac Caul, 15.

Mac Kage, 122. Mac Kaghone, 86. Mac Kague, 122. Mac Kaige, 122. Mac Kaigue, 122. Mac Karee, 83. Mac Karrye, 83. Mac Kay, 73. Mac Keag, 122. Mac Keague, 122. Mac Keany, 85. Mac Keary, 83. Mac Kee, 73. Mac Keegan, 39. Mac Keeman, 44. Mac Keemon, 44. Mac Keever, 84. Mac Keevor, 84. Mac Keige, 122. Mac Kellen, 85. Mac Kena, 85. Mac Kenay, 85. Mac Kenery, 82. Mac Keneyry, 82. Mac Keniry, 82. Mac Kenna, 85. Mac Kennery, 82. Mac Kenny, 85. Mac Keo, 64. Mac Keoan, 85. Mac Keogh, 64. Mac Keon, 85. Mac Keone, 85. Mac Keough, 48, 64. Mac Keown, 85. Mac Kerlie, 28. Mac Kerley, 28. Mac Kernan, 66. Mac Kerry, 83. Mac Kever, 84. Mac Kevor, 84. Mac Kewer, 84. Mac Key, 73. Mac Kibbon, 44. Mac Kiernan, 66. Mac Kiever, 84. Mac Kilan, 85. Mac Killbride, 50. Mac Killegode, 80. Mac Killen, 85. Mac Killigott, 80. Mac Kilveen, 91. Mac Kimmons, 44. Mac King, 74. Mac Kinn, 74. Mac Kinna, 85. Mac Kinch, 1. Mac Kinerkin, 82. Mac Kinnertin, 82. Mac Kinney, 85. Mac Kinny, 85. Mac Kirdy, 79. Mac Kiver, 84. Mac Kneight, 88. Mac Knight, 67, 88. Mac Knulty, 88. Mac Kone, 85. Mac Kough, 64. Mac Krevie, 84. Mac Kurdy, 79.

Mac Lean, 85. Mac Leland, 78. Mac Lellan, 78. Mac Leroy, 52. Mac Lester, 77. Mac Levin, 36. Mac Lochlin, 85. Mac Loghlin, 85. Mac Loone, 83. Mac Loughlin, 85. Mac Lune, 83. Mac Lysaght, 74.

Mac Machan, 86. Mac Machon, 86. Mac Maghen, 86. Mac Maghon, 86. Mac Maghone, 86. Mac Maghowney, 86. Mac Mahan, · 86. Mac Mahon, 86. Mac Mahowna, 86. Mac Mann, 86. Mac Manis, 86. Mac Manish, 86. Mac Manus, 86. Mac Maurice, 44. Mac Mearty, 79. Mac Merty, 79. Mac Millan, 87. Mac Millen, 87. Mac Moenassa, 86. Mac Mordie, 79. Mac Morish, 44. Mac Moroghoe, 86. Mac Morris, 44. Mac Mowllane, 87. Mac Moylan, 87. Mac Mullan, 87. Mac Mullen, 87. Mac Mullin, 87. Mac Mullon, 87. Mac Murdy, 79. Mac Murphewe, 86. Mac Murroghowe, 86. Mac Murrough, 86. Mac Murrow, 86. Mac Murtery, 79. Mac Murtrie, 79. Mac Murtry, 79. Mac Mearty, 79.

Mac Naghten, 88. Mac Naghton, 88. Mac Nairn, 82. Mac Nama, 87. Mac Namara, 87. Mac Namarra, 87. Mac Namarrow, 87. Mac Namee, 87. Mac Naryn, 82. Mac Naught, 88. Mac Naughton, 88. Mac Nally, 87. Mac Neaghtane, 88. Mac Neal, 88. Mac Neese, 1. Mac Neight, 88. Mac Neile, 88. Mac Neill, 88. Mac Neiry, 82. Mac Nema, 87. Mac Nerhenny, 82. Mac Nern, 82. Mac Nerney, 82. Mac Nertney, 82. Mac Niece, 1. Mac Night, 88. Mac Nirney, 82. Mac Nish, 1. Mac Nite, 88. Mac Nulty, 88. Mac Nutt, 125.

Mac Owen, 85.

Mac Padgen, 82. Mac Paden, 82. Mac Paddan, 82. Mac Padden, 82. Mac Padian, 82. Mac Padine, 82. Mac Paidin, 82. Mac Paul, 110. Mac Phadden, 82. Mac Phail, 110. Mac Poland, 110. Mac Polin, 110. Mac Poyle, 110.

Mac Queen, 89. Mac Quilly, 24.

Mac Ray, 79. Mac Rea, 79. Mac Reavy, 84. Mac Redmond, 113. Mac Roary, 114. Mac Rory, 114. Mac Rudderie, 67.

Mac Seveney, 89. Mac Shaen, 88. Mac Shaine, 88. Mac Shan, 88. Mac Shane, 88. Mac Shanley, 117. Mac Sheain, 88. Mac Sheane, 88. Mac Sheehy, 89, 118. Mac Sween, 89. Mac Sweeney, 89. Mac Swine, 89. Mac Swiney, 89.

Mac Tague, 122. Mac Tamney, 122. Mac Teague, 122. Mac Teigue, 122. Mac Tigue, 122. Mac Timney, 122.

Mac Vail, 110. Mac Varry, 83. Mac Vay, 89. Mac Vea, 89. Mac Veagh, 89. Mac Veigh, 89. Mac Verry, 83. Mac Vey, 89.

Mac Ward, 124. Mac Wray, 79.

McAbreham, 7. McAckolly, 24. McAlaster, 77. McAnchelly, 24. McAnna, 78. McAncrossane, 27. McArtan, 78. McArtane, 78.

McBrehon, 7. McBrehuna, 7. McBrodie, 8. McBrouddie, 8. McBroudy, 8.

McCaba, 77. McCaele, 77. McCahey, 48. McCallerie, 112. McCalreaghe, 112. McCalreogh, 112. McCanna, 78. McCartane, 78. McCashin, 14. McCassin, 14. McCaugh-

O Farrissa, 43. O Faughy, 40. O Faye, 40. O Fearguise, 43. O Feehan, 42. O Fenane, 41. O Fenegane, 43. O Feolane, 42. O Fergus, 43. O Ferrally, 41. O Ferris, 43. O Feilly, 42. O Fighane, 42. O Fihillie, 42. O Fihily, 42. O Finane, 41. O Finegane, 43. O Finisey, 43. O Finnee, 42. O Finn, 43. O Finne, 43. O Finny, 42. O Fionn, 43. O Flagherty, 45. O Flaherty, 45. O Flahie, 45. O Flahiff, 45. O Flanagan, 45. O Flannagaine, 45. O Flannelly, 46. O Flannylla, 46. O Floine, 46. O Floinge, 46. O Flynn, 46. O Foedy, 120. O Fogarty, 46. O Fogerty, 46. O Folane, 42. O Foley, 47. O Folowe, 47. O Foodie, 120. O Foody, 120. O Forane, 47. O Forehan, 47. O Forehane, 47. O Forhan, 47. O Forhane, 47. O Fourhan, 47. O Fowrane, 47. O Fuarayne, 47. O Fylan, 42. O Fynea, 42.

O Gaeney, 47. O Gallagher, 48. O Galleghure, 48. O Gannon, 48. O Ganon, 48. O Gara, 50. O Garey, 50. O Garien, 49. O Garry, 50. O Garvey, 49. O Garvie, 49. O Garvin, 49. O Gavan, 49. O Geary, 50. O Geiry, 50. O Gibbelaun, 50. O Gibbellayne, 50. O Gibbon, 44. O Gillane, 52. O Gillain, 52. O Gillegan, 52. O Gilgan, 52. O Glassane, 53. O Glesaine, 53. O Gleasan, 53. O Goonerie, 47. O Gooney, 47. O Gorman, 53. O Gormeley, 53. O Gormley, 53. O Gorumley, 53. O Gownain, 47. O Gownane, 47. O Gowney, 47. O Gownro, 47. O Grada, 104. O Grady, 104. O Greefa, 54. O Griffy, 54. O Grighie, 54. O Grimley, 53. O Grogaine, 54. O Growgane, 54. O Guindelane, 111.

O Hagerty, 55. O Hagher, 103. O Haghie, 103. O Hagirtie, 55. O Hahir, 103. O Haire, 103. O Hairt, 101. O Halfpenny, 56. O Hallaghan, 55. O Hallaran, 55. O Halleghane, 55. O Halleran, 55. O Halleron, 55. O Halloraine, 55. O Halloran, 55. O Hallyn, 1. O Halowrane, 55. O Halpenny, 56. O Halpin, 56. O Hanain, 57. O Handlon, 56. O Hanigan, 56. O Hanlee, 56. O Hanley, 56. O Hanlone, 56. O Hanlowne, 56. O Hannaine, 57. O Hannegan, 56. O Hanrahan, 57. O Hara, 105. O Haraghtane, 57. O Haran, 59. O Hare, 103. O Harra, 105. O Harragan, 57. O Harran, 59. O Harrane, 59. O Harrington, 57. O Hart, 101. O Harte, 101. Hartigan, 58. O Harvey, 58. O Hayllane, 60. O Hay, 59. O Hays, 59. O Hea, 59. O Headen, 58. O Headyne, 58. O Heagane, 62. O Heagertie, 55. O Heaken, 62. O Healane, 60. O Healie, 59. O Healy, 59. O Heanagane, 59. O Heanesey, 60. O Heany, 59. O Heden, 58. O Hederiman, 108. O Hederscoll, 38. O Hedian, 58. O Hedine, 58. O Hegane, 62. O Hegertie, 55. O Hehir, 103. O Hein, 61. O Helane, 60. O Hely, 59. O Henane, 59. O Henegane, 59. O Heney, 59. O Henly, 56. O Hennaine, 59. O Hennessy, 60. O Hensey, 60. O Heolane, 60. O Herraghton, 57. O Herlehy, 60. O Herlihy, 60. O Hern, 59. O Heron, 59. O Hevine, 40. O Hewe, 59. O Heyden, 58. O Heyne, 61. O Hickee, 62. O Hickey, 62. O Hidirscoll, 38. O Hierlehy, 60. O Higane, 62. O Hiffernan, 60. O Hifferane, 60. O Hiffernan, 60. O Higane, 62. O Higgins, 62. O Hilane, 60. O Hillane, 60. O Hine, 61. O Hoa, 58. O Hoasy, 62. O Hogan, 61. O Hogaine, 61. O Hogane, 61. O Hogertie, 46. O Hohy, 58. O Holane, 60. O Hollan, 60. O Holland, 60. O Holegane, 61. O Holehan, 61. O Honie, 54. O Hoolan, 60. O Horan, 61. O Horgane, 57. O Horigane, 57. O Horsike, 12. O Horogan, 57. O Hosey, 62. O Hossy, 62. O Houlighane, 61. O Houlihan, 61. O Hourigan, 57. O Hourihan, 57. O Howny, 54. O Hownyn, 54. O Howrane, 57. O Hoye, 58. O Huggin, 62. O Hugh, 59. O Huky, 58. O Hunnyn, 54. O Hurrane, 61. O Hurrone, 61. O Hylane, 60. O Hyne, 61.

O Kaane, 10. O Kahane, 10. O Kane, 10. O Karr, 14. O Keallaghir, 64. O Keally, 64. O Kealy, 64. O Keane, 10. O Kearane, 11. O Kearney, 13. O Keating, 63. O Keaty, 63. O Keavane, 15. O Keefe, 64. O Keeve, 64. O Kegly, 111. O Kelliher, 64. O Kelly, 65. O Kenaith, 66. O Kenna, 66. O Kennavain, 12. O Kenneally, 65. O Kennedy, 65. O Kennellan, 111. O Kennelly, 65. O Kenny, 66. O Kenolan, 111. O Kerby, 67. O Kerevan, 67. O Kerigane, 66. O Kermody, 13. O Kerrane, 11. O Kerrywane, 67. O Kerry, 13. O Kervick, 67. O Kervy, 67. O Kerwick, 67. O Kevane, 15. O Kibbon, 44. O Kieran, 11. O Kierrigain, 66. O Kine, 24. O Kineally, 65. O Kinedy, 65. O Kineghan, 28. O Kinna, 66. O Kirry, 13. O Kirwan, 67. O Knavin, 98. O Knawsie, 98. O Knee, 98. O Kuddyhy, 27. O Kueily, 64. O Kurnane, 24. O Kynaghan, 28. O Kynsillaghe, 66.

O Lagan, 72. O Lagane, 72. O Laghlan, 104. O Laghnane, 71. O Lalor, 68. O Lalour, 68. O Lane, 68. O Lanegane, 69. O Langan, 69. O Langane, 69. O Lanigan, 69. O Lannan, 69. O Lannegan, 69. O Laven, 69. O Lavin, 69. O Lavine, 69. O Lawler, 68. O Laynan, 72. O Layne, 68. O Laynen, 72. O Leaghan, 70. O Leaghy, 70. O Leavy, 70. O Leane, 68. O Leary, 70. O Lee, 70. O Leahane, 70. O Lenaghan, 71. O Leneghan, 71. O Lennane, 69, 71. O Lennan, 71. O Lensie, 71. O Leye, 70. O Leynam, 72. O Leyne, 68. O Leynen, 72. O Lie, 70. O Lien, 68. O Lochan, 72. O Logan, 72. O Logher, 72. O Loghlan, 104. O Loghlen, 104. O Loghnane, 71. O Loghrane, 72. O Lonagan, 69. O Lonan, 69. O Lonane, 69. O Londregan, 72. O Lonegan, 69. O Lonergane, 72.

O Talheighe, 121. O Talty, 121. O Tearney, 121. O Ternane, 121. O Tiernan, 121. O Tierney, 121. O Tierny, 121. O Toole, 109. O Toomey, 122. O Toughill, 109. O Touhill, 109. O Towell, 109. O Towie, 123. O Trasey, 124. O Trassy, 124. O Tressy, 124. O Trevir, 123. O Trover, 123. O Otterson, 23. O Tuale, 109. O Twohill, 109. O Twohy 123. O Twomey, 122.

O'Whalen, 42. O'Whealane, 42. Owen, 85. Owens, 85.

Padden, 82. Paddison. 82. Padian, 82. Patten, 82. Patterson, 82. Pattinson, 82. Pattison, 82. Paulson, 110. Payton, 82. Pender, 110. Pendergast, 110. Pendergrass, 110. Phelan, 42. Philan, 42. Pinder, 110. Plonket, 109. Plunket, 109. Plunkett, 109. Poer, 110. Poland, 110. Polin, 110. Polson, 110. Poole, 110. Poor, 110. Porcell, 110. Powel, 110. Powell, 54, 110. Power, 110. Powlson, 110. Prendergast, 110. Prindergast, 110. Purcell, 110. Purcill, 110. Pursell, 110. Purshell, 110.

Quaid, 111. Quaile, 111. Quaine, 111. Quan, 111. Quane, 111. Quann, 111. Quealy, 64. Queely, 64. Queen, 123. Querk, 112. Quiddihy, 27. Quigley, 111. Quill, 111. Quilligan, 18. Quin, 123. Quinlan, 111. Quinlivan, 111. Quinn, 123. Quirk, 112. Quirke, 112.

Ractigan, 112. Raftery, 112. Ratican, 112. Ratigan, 112. Rattigan, 112. Ravy, 112. Ray, 112. Rea, 79, 112. Really, 107. Realy, 107. Reardan, 113. Reardon, 113. Reavey, 112. Redahan, 113. Reddan, 113. Reddin, 113. Reddington, 113. Redehan, 113. Redington, 113. Reddy, 113. Redmond, 113. Reely, 107. Reen, 115. Regan, 106. Reid, 112. Reigh, 112. Reilly, 107. Rewan, 114. Rhategan, 112. Rhatigan, 112. Rielly, 107. Riley, 107. Rinn, 115. Ring, 115. Riordan, 113. Roache, 114. Roan, 114. Roane, 114. Roche, 114. Rodden, 113. Rodan, 113. Rodaughan, 113. Roddy, 113. Roden, 113. Rodgers, 114. Rodin, 113. Rogan, 114. Rogers, 114. Rogerson, 114. Roghtigan, 112. Ronan, 115. Ronane, 115. Ronayne, 115. Roney, 115. Roon, 114. Rooney, 115. Rorison, 114. Rorke, 107. Rosel, 115. Rossell, 115. Rouane, 114. Rourke, 107. Rowan, 114. Rowney, 115. Roy, 52. Royan, 114. Ruan, 114. Ruane, 114. Rudden, 113. Ruddon, 113. Ruddy, 113. Rudican, 113. Rudihan, 113. Rush, 72. Rushell, 115. Russell, 115. Ryder, 77. Ryan, 107. Rynn, 115.

Salmon, 5.

Scallon, 116. Scally, 116. Scandlon, 116. Scanlan, 116. Scanlon, 116. Scannell, 116. Scully, 116. Seeny, 117. Seerey, 117. Seery, 117. Seward, 120. Sexton, 116. Shanaghan, 117. Shanahan, 117. Shanan, 117. Shane, 88. Shanihan, 117. Shanley, 117. Shannagh, 117. Shannessy, 108. Shannon, 117. Shanny, 117. Shanon, 117. Shaughnessy, 108. Shasnan, 116. Shea, 108. Sheals, 119. Shean, 118. Shee, 108. Sheahan, 118. Sheean, 118. Sheedy, 118. Sheehan, 118. Sheehy, 89, 118. Sheen, 118. Sheilds, 119. Shiels, 119. Sheils, 119. Sheny, 117. Sheoye, 63. Sheridan, 118. Sherridan, 118. Shields, 119. Shiels, 119. Shiles, 119. Shinagh, 117. Shinnick, 117. Shinnock, 117. Shinwick, 117. Sheye, 63. Shunny, 117. Silk, 118. Simmons, 44. Simons, 44. Skelly, 116. Slamon, 119. Slavin, 119. Slattery, 119. Sleavin, 119. Sleevin, 119. Slevan, 119. Slevin, 119. Sloan, 119. Sloane, 119. Sloey, 119. Slone, 119. Slowey, 119. Slown, 119. Sloy, 119. Sloyan, 119. Sloyne, 119. Smallen, 120. Smith, 84. Smollan, 120. Smullen, 120. Smyth, 84. Somers, 120. Sommers, 120. Soolivan, 109. Spalane, 120. Speed, 120. Spellane, 120. Spellman, 120. Spelman, 120. Spillane, 120. Splane, 120. Splaine, 120. Spollan, 120. Spollane, 120. Staney, 32. Sullevan, 109. Sullivan, 109. Summers, 120. Sweeney, 89. Swift, 120. Swiney, 89. Sword, 120. Swords, 120. Symonds, 44.

Tague, 122. Talbot, 121. Talbote, 121. Talebot, 121. Tally, 121. Talty, 121. Tamney, 122. Taulty, 121. Teague, 122. Teige, 122. Teigue, 122. Tempeny, 122. Tenpeny, 122. Terney, 121. Ternan, 121. Terrance, 28. Terry, 28. Tiernan, 121. Tierney, 121. Tighe, 122. Tigue, 122. Tilly, 121. Timony, 122. Timpany, 122. Toal, 109. Toale, 109. Tobin, 122. Tobine, 122. Tobyn, 122. Tohall, 109. Tohill, 109. Tooey, 123. Toohill, 109. Toohy, 123. Toole, 109. Toomey, 122. Toompane, 122. Touhy, 123. Torley, 28. Toughill, 109. Towell, 109. Towey, 123. Towmey, 122. Tracey, 124. Tracy, 124. Trassy, 124. Travers, 123. Travors, 123. Treacy, 124. Tressy, 124. Trevors, 123. Treyor, 123. Trower, 123. Tuhy, 123. Tully, 46, 121. Tumpany, 122. Tuohill, 109. Tuohy, 123. Tuomy, 122. Turley, 28. Twigley, 111. Twohill, 109. Twohy, 123. Twomey, 122. Twoohy, 123. Twoomey, 122. Tymmany, 122. Tympany, 122.

Vadin, 82. Vahy, 89. Vail, 110. Vaughan, 92. Veigh, 89. Vesey, 89. Voghane, 92.

Walsh, 123. Walshe, 123. Ward, 124. Warren, 105. Waters, 12. Watters, 12. Whelan, 42. White, 124. Whyte, 124. Wren, 115. Wrenn, 115. Wrynn, 115.